Values in Social Work

Michael Horne

ᗅSHGATE

COMMUNITY
CARE
THE INDEPENDENT VOICE OF SOCIAL WORK

To Liz, Megan and Cerian

First Edition published in 1987 by
Wildwood House Ltd

This reprint published by
Ashgate
Ashgate Publishing Ltd
Gower House, Croft Road
Aldershot, Hants GU11 3HR
England

Ashgate Publishing Company
Old Post Road
Brookfield, Vermont 05036
USA

Reprinted 1993

British Library Cataloguing in Publication Data

Horne, Michael
    Values in social work. – (Community care practice handbooks; 26).
    1. Social service – Great Britain – Moral and ethical aspects.
    2. Values
    I. Title   II. Series
    361.3'01'3   HV245

Library of Congress Cataloging-in-Publication Data

Horne, Michael. 1953–
    Values in social care. – (Community care practice handbooks; 26).
    Bibliography: p.
    1. Social service – Moral and ethical aspects.
    2. Social service – Great Britain.
    I. Title   II. Series.
    HV40.H66   1988   361'.941   87-21123

ISBN 1 85742 161 2   1708580

Printed and bound in Great Britain by
Biddles Ltd, Guildford and King's Lynn

**Community Care
Practice Handbooks**

General Editor: Martin Davies

Values in Social Work

Community Care
Practice Handbooks

General Editor: Martin Davies

Contents

Acknowledgements

I would like to thank the six social workers who kindly agreed to be interviewed, and whose contribution plays a central part in this book. For reasons of confidentiality, they cannot be named. I would also like to express my gratitude to Professor Martin Davies and Doctor David Howe for the support and encouragement that they gave to me whilst I was at the University of East Anglia.

Preface

In recent years there has been an increasing number of books published on social work values. Most of them give good theoretical expositions of what these values are, and what they mean, in varying degrees of philosophical and sociological complexity.

In *Values in Social Work*, whilst starting with a description and discussion of social work values from a theoretical perspective, the overall emphasis is very much on understanding these values from the perspective of local authority-based social work practice. There are several reasons for this.

First, my own social work practice (residential and field-based) continually generated questions related to values in social work, such as why the idea of client self-determination does not always seem to be very prominent (if recognizable at all) in practice. Philosophically based texts told me a great deal about the concept of self-determination, but little or nothing about its relevance and place in actual social work practice.

Second, and closely related to the first reason, is the need to examine practice, to understand what the social workers do, and *why* they do it. As a social worker, what I did often did not seem to accord with the textbooks (perhaps a reflection on my practice as much as a comment on the textbooks). The 'reality' often was much more complex, with more variables, possibilities and restrictions.

These two reasons put together, I think, explain why I saw a need for and engaged in a study of values in social work from a 'practice'-based perspective.

My study originally emerged as a thesis for the Master of Social Work degree (University of East Anglia). The presentation of the study here largely keeps to the thesis form as it offers, as far as I can see, a logical and systematic investigation into values in social work practice.

Introduction

A value determines what a person thinks he ought to do, which may not be the same as what he wants to do, or what it is in his interests to do, or what in fact he actually does. Values in this sense give rise to general standards and ideals by which we judge our own and others' conduct; they also give rise to specific obligations (CCETSW, 1976, p. 14).

Social work is a professional activity. Implicit in its practice are ethical principles which prescribe the professional responsibility of the social worker. The primary objective of the code of ethics is to make these implicit principles explicit for the protection of clients (BASW, 1976).

Social workers have religiously clung to values . . . and have not done these values justice. We seem to cling to them intuitively, out of faith, as a symbol of our humanitarianism. We have not treated them with the seriousness befitting their role as a fulcrum of practice (Vigilante, 1974).

Social work as a value-laden activity
Social work as an activity, and as far as its knowledge base (derived from the social sciences) is concerned, is a value-laden activity. Despite the skills which it espouses as affording it 'technical' or 'scientific' validity, they do not remove within its practice the necessity of making evaluative judgements and decisions.

Without entering into the heated controversy over the degree of objectivity in the social sciences, all would surely agree that in the case of social work, a value system, (more often than not couched in terms of social and political ideology) forms the general framework of decision making within which the social worker defines both his overall role and his specific course of action (Pritchard and Taylor, 1978, p. 70).

To seek and yearn for an expertise in human relationships, as Downie and Telfer argue, with the aim of denying the 'value-reality' of social work is illusory: 'No amount of knowledge of what is the case can ever establish for us what we ought to do about it' (Downie and Telfer, 1980, p. 22).

Levy (1976, p. 238) also describes social work as a value-based pro-fession, when he describes social work as 'not only a way of doing something, but a constellation of preferences concerning what merits doing and how it should be done . . . . '

'Value talk' in social work

Timms (1983, p. 24), refers to three main ways in which social work values are written about. First, they appear in the form of generalized accounts of 'value' or 'values' (for example, Biestek, 1961). Second, they are the subject of essays (or collections of essays) in which some critical assessment is attempted of a 'value' or 'values' (for example, McDermott, 1975). Third, they may be subject to some form of empirical investigation, which studies social work values in a more direct manner (for example, McLeod and Meyer, 1967).

Both the 'literature'-based approach, and the 'empirically' based approach have been criticized for their tendency to fall into the trap of routinely listing what are taken to be social work values, and for their lack of conceptual analysis of the nature and form of these values.

Levy (1973) has written of:

> the tendency in social work literature to list routinely and indiscriminately a series of so-called social work values as if nothing more need to be said for all to understand . . . They [social workers] are so accustomed to citing these items, almost by rote, that no explanation seems necessary – and certainly not from one another. This may be one of the reasons for the limited progress in coping with professional value issues.

Similarly, Timms (1983) criticizes the social work literature for not treating the subject of social work values, and 'values' problems with sufficient 'rigour' and 'conceptualization':

> 'Value' appears frequently in social work literature, but value talk is underdeveloped and conversation about values or social work values has hardly started. This is mainly because it is assumed that everyone knows what values (or beliefs, or ethics, or philosophy, or attitudes, or preferences) are; that is, a value is a value; and that values may be elaborated, but cannot be argued about (Timms, 1983, p. 32).

Empirical research on social work values has also been criticized for its tendency to compile lists and for its inadequate attention to con-ceptual analysis of the values it lists. Research studies into social work values have not been numerous, the most well known being that of Pumphrey (1959), McLeod and Meyer (1967), and Channon (1974).

Timms (1983, p. 28) describes such empirical work that has so far been carried out as 'premature in so far as its grasp on "value" is hesitant and clumsy'. In his critisism of Pumphrey and McLeod and Meyer he argues that both lack 'conceptual exploration'. For example, regarding McLeod and Meyer's research, he writes, 'It is not easy to avoid the judgement that more conceptual preparation would have produced a better result' (1983, p. 28). With respect to Pumphrey's research, he argues that he failed to analyse possible problems and conflicts inherent in the application of values in practice.

> Protective activity might sometimes clash with the client's right of self-determination, whilst suffering could be said to be part of the 'reality' which social workers quite often believe they should assist their clients to face (1970, p. 120).

Timms goes on to suggest that what is needed is a study of social work values, based on what social workers actually do when faced with a choice between 'valued' courses of action, rather than studies based on what social workers mention or list as being important: 'The question to task is not so much what things, concepts, states of affairs, do social workers value, but how much do they value them?' (1970, p. 120). Similarly in 1983 (p. 32) he writes: 'we should just attend more closely and critically to the literature and also to the problems of the social worker making choices.'

BASW and CCETSW

This lack of critical examination and conceptual analysis of social work values is also evident in BASW's (British Association of Social Workers) *A Code of Ethics for Social Work* (1975), and in the paper on training in social work (January 1985) from CCETSW (Central Council for Education and Training in Social Work). The opening statement of BASW's *Code of Ethics* (quoted at the beginning of the Introduction) raises two immediate problems or questions.

First by stating at the outset that, 'social work is a professional activity', it seems to ignore an important point (made by Fairbairn, 1985, p. 86), that a set of ethical principles for social work should start with a consideration (or at least an acknowledgement) of the responsibilities of the social worker. In the *Code* this 'unqualified' description of social work as a 'profession' is followed up by a call for a code of ethics 'for the protection of clients'. It could be argued that social work as a profession is severely limited, because certainly in Britain, it is mostly practised within local authority organizations, and social workers are accountable to the authority of their employers, rather than to their clients for their decisions. If, as Payne (1985, p. 102) argues, a code of ethics is based on the idea of professional responsibility to, and for the protection of clients, how can it, and does it, also accommodate responsibility to an employer?

To be fair, the *Code* does recognize this 'dilemma' by stating in paragraph 3 that social workers are responsible to 'their clients, to their employers, to each other, to colleagues in other disciplines, and to society'. Also, in paragraph 4 of the commentary, it states that it is an oversimplification to say that either clients or employers should take precedence. However, the effect of this recognition is to add to the confusion and lack of clarity (particularly as it is supposed to be a 'code' of ethics), because the latter two statements contradict the original statement that the 'primary objective of the code is to prescribe rules for the protection of clients'. Nor does the code suggest how possible conflicts of interest and responsibility which the social worker might face, be resolved. From this, it does seem that as a guide for practice, the code is inadequate, even at a very general level.

In the paper issued by CCETSW (paper 20.3, January, 1985) on training in social work, it is stated that:

> It is fundamental that education and training leading to a qualification award should aim to equip social workers with the professional values and ethics which must guide their work and their accountability, and which they need in order to act as part of a wider professional group. Given that at present most social workers in this country are employed in public services, the nature and purposes of which are by definition politically determined, it is important that qualifying education and training should provide the opportunity for social work students to learn about the roles and responsibilities of professionals employed in public, voluntary, and private bureaucratic structures, and to be clear about the values and ethics espoused by their profession.

Once again, this is a confused and evasive statement, primarily in that it offers no recognition of the possibility of conflict between 'social work values and ethics', to which it says social workers are accountable, and their employers, whose 'nature and purposes are "politically determined" '. It is important for social workers to be 'clear about the values and ethics espoused by their profession', but the statement does not indicate what these values and ethics actually are.

Both of these examples, from BASW and CCETSW support the argument that much of the 'value talk' in and about social work suffers seriously from a lack of conceptual analysis of the values it espouses, and is evasive of possible value conflicts and problems in social work practice, often hiding behind the ill-defined notion of 'professional'.

Aims

The aim of the book is to examine the main social work values, what they are, what they mean, and understand them in the context of local authority-based social work (as this is the context in which most social workers work in Britain). This is done in three parts.

Part I consists of a critical examination of the social work 'value' literature, concentrating on the values of 'respect for persons' and client 'self-determination'.

Part II consists of a small-scale empirical study of what happens to values in social work practice. In relation to Timms' comments quoted earlier, the study aims to show, by describing and analysing cases in detail, what social workers do, and how their values 'work' in practice. Whilst Part I focuses on the relationship between the social worker and the client, Part II looks particularly at how that relationship is determined and affected by 'outside factors', for example, by the demands of agency function and society's expectations.

Part III follows on from this by presenting a theoretical framework which gives a description of social work that accommodates and examines the nature of the social worker's relationships with both the individual and with society, and offers an understanding of social work values in this context. Part III attempts to analyse and clarify what are often left in 'value talk' as vague (or in the case of BASW's *Code of Ethics*, contradictory as well) references to the social worker's responsibilities to individuals (clients) and to society.

PART I
VALUES IN THEORY

As mentioned in the Introduction, 'value-talk' in social work often consists of lists of what it is considered the moral or ethical principles of social work are, or should be. Whilst the lists vary, there are generally strong similarities between them. Timms (1983, p. 43) gives five typical inclusions in a 'value list':

1 To respect the client.
2 To accept 'him' for 'himself'.
3 Not to condemn 'him'.
4 To uphold 'his' right to self-determination.
5 To respect 'his' confidence.

Butrym (1976, chap. 3) describes three fundamental assumptions on which social work is based:

1 Respect for persons.
2 'A belief in the social nature of man as a unique creature depending on other men for fulfillment of his uniqueness'.
3 'A belief in the human capacity for change, growth and betterment'.

From these 'values of a very high order of abstraction' (p. 47) she then lists six 'middle-range conceptualisations of moral principles' that are directly relevant to social work practice. These are based on Biestek's classification (1961):

1 Acceptance.
2 Non-judgemental attitude.
3 Individualization.
4 The 'purposeful expression of feelings' and 'controlled emotional involvement'.
5 Confidentiality.
6 Self-determination.

The analysis below concentrates on 'respect for persons'. Basically all other values are derived from, and are a part of the meaning of this moral principle. This will be followed by an analysis of the value 'the client's right to self-determination', which is one of the central principles (as far as social work is concerned) that is derived from 'respect for persons', and which is also one of the most contentious and open to debate regarding its applicability (and limits) in contemporary social work practice.

From the brief lists offered above, this approach most obviously ignores (at least explicitly) the value of 'respecting the client's confidence', which appears in Timms' and Butrym's lists, and also number (4) from Butrym's 'middle-range' list. All the other values are expressions of 'respect of persons' and 'client self-determination', which itself indicates the centrality of these two values in providing a value-base to social work. It is because of this that the following analysis of the social work 'value' literature and theory concentrates on these two values.

1 Respect for Persons

The concept of 'respect for persons' is fundamental to most discussions of values in social work literature, both as a moral principle from which other principles are derived, and as a prerequisite for morality itself. One of the most influential writers on social work values has been Raymond Plant, who describes respect for persons as: 'not just a moral principle, on the contrary it is a presupposition of having the concept of a moral principle at all' (Plant, 1970, p. 20). Plant goes on to say that other values such as self-determination are implicit in 'respect for persons' (I will discuss whether or not this is the case in the next chapter). Downie and Telfer, two other influential writers on social work values, go even further than Plant when they say that:

> the attitude of 'respect for persons' is morally basic . . . . not only is it the paramount moral attitude, but also . . . . all other moral principles and attitudes are to be explained in terms of it (Downie and Telfer, 1969, p.33).

As far as its fundamental importance to social work practice is concerned, the following quote from BASW illustrates what it sees to be the practical implications of 'respect for persons':

> basic to the profession of social work is the recognition of the value and dignity of every human being irrespective of origin status, sex, age, belief or contribution to society. The profession accepts responsibility to encourage and facilitate the self-realisation of the individual person with due regard for the interest of others (BASW 1975).

Plant himself indicates that in relation to social work practice, the values of individualization, acceptance, and self-direction (determination) are in fact implicit in 'respect for persons': 'They are deductions from this concept in that they are part of its very meaning. Respect for persons is, on this view, the basic value of casework' (Plant, 1970, p.11).

Ends and means
The most common way of describing what is meant by this concept is that people should be treated as ends in themselves, not as means to

ends, which comes directly from the Kantian maxim that one should:

> Act in such a way that you always treat humanity, whether in your own person or in the person of any other, never simply as a means, but always at the same time as an end (Kant, I in Paton, 1949, p. 91).

The concept that each person is an end in him/herself argues for an equal evaluation of each individual which is not based on what are considered to be morally arbitrary features such as experience, ability, intelligence, social standing, or any other 'empirical' quality. Whilst every individual possesses a number of such features which help to determine his/her role in society; in themselves, these do not constitute his/her value as an end. According to 'respect for persons' such variations are arbitrary and exist on 'top of' the evaluation that each person has 'a legitimate claim to be valued equally with any others' (Budgen 1982, p. 34).

Zofia Butrym describes 'respect for persons' as being 'due to the inherent worth of man and is thus independent of his actual achievements or behaviour' (Butrym, 1976, p. 43).

Plant sums up this philosophy in the following quotation from Kant which he cites:

> A man deserves respect as a potential moral agent in terms of his transcendental characteristic, not because of a particular con-junction of empirical qualities which he might possess. Traits of character might command admiration and other such responses, but respect is owed to a man irrespective of what he does because he is a man (Plant 1970, p. 12).

In other words, to treat someone as an end is to treat him/her as being of unconditional moral worth.

Rationality

The basis of, or justification for 'respect for persons' is, according to Kant, man's possession of rationality – the rational will. Before des-cribing this, it should be pointed out that 'rationality' is not to be taken as being contrasted with 'irrationality', but with 'non-rationality'. For example, many clients come or are sent to see social workers because they are considered not to be behaving rationally. This does not mean that they are to be regarded as being irrational – rather that their ability to make rational decisions may be temp-orarily affected or lessened through some form of stress, crisis, ill-ness etc. The case of children, mentally handicapped or mentally ill people is more complex and will be discussed in the examination below of what and who constitutes a person (or 'personhood').

According to Kant, an individual's absolute worth comes from his/ her possession of rationality - the rational will. It is the rational will that enables one to think and act in a rational manner.

Budgen describes two ways in which the exercise of the 'rational will' can be seen, first by 'the ability to choose for oneself, and more extensively to formulate purposes, plans and policies of one's own' (Budgen 1982, p. 34); and second, by 'the ability to carry out decisions, plans or policies without undue reliance on the help of others' (quote from Downie and Telfer, 1969, p. 20).

To impair a person's abilities to choose and execute his/her own plan is, as Downie and Telfer put it, 'to that extent to destroy him as a person' (1969, p. 21).

Autonomy
The main feature of Kant's analysis of the 'rational will' is the auto-nomy of the will - that is, our ability to act in the pursuit of our own self-chosen goals - to act in pursuit of our own personal conception of the 'good life'. Within our liberal, democratic (relatively so at least) society, autonomy is valued very highly, both as a means to the achievement of other goals and as an end in its own right. As Budgen and Downie and Telfer have pointed out, people have their own chosen purposes and projects, so to treat someone as an end is to recognize the individual's right to live according to his/her purposes and projects.

To treat someone solely as a 'means' would for example, be to make a false promise to them in order to secure a loan which one had no intention of repaying.

Richard Lindley (1984) cites Aldous Huxley's novel, *Brave New World*, as an example of a society in which the majority of the people were without any autonomy, that is, they were not treated as ends in themselves. Rather, they were treated instrumentally, that is, their wills were manipulated, allegedly for their own benefit. Therefore, pleasant though the *Brave New World* may have been for its inhabitants, it nevertheless seriously violated the Kantian principle of 'respect for persons'.

It is important to be aware that each person, as the possessor of a rational will is able to live according to his/her own projects, purposes and rules, but another person may possibly live according to a different set of projects and rules. So whilst it may be morally accept-able to use rational argument to try and get the other person to change his/her mind, it would be morally wrong (a denial of him/her as a person) to attempt to make him/her change their mind by the exercise of power, coercion or manipulation. On a strict interpre-tation of the Kantian principle, as rational beings, we should always respect the autonomy of others. To do otherwise would be morally wrong, since the principle which justified the behaviour could not be accepted by the other person or persons, and therefore could not be 'willed to be a universal law'. The CCETSW paper on values in social work puts this in the following way:

> A rational being cannot propose to act on a principle if he cannot propose at the same time that others should act upon it. Man should be seen as an end in himself; to use a person as a means by deceiving or manipulating him is to deprive him of the respect and opportunity for choice which one would expect for oneself (CCETSW 1976, p. 22).

The obvious social work value which has its roots in this aspect of 'respect for persons' is the concept of self-determination – the ability to choose for oneself, and the ability to carry out actions and policies etc. of one's own. (I shall discuss this value/concept in detail in the next chapter.)

A further aspect of 'respecting a person', also mentioned in the CCETSW paper on values (1976, p. 29), involves an awareness that certain roles, projects, values etc. apply to everyone alike, for example, social workers and their clients. So, in helping with a client's problems, the social worker is morally bound not to do so at the expense of the social norms which apply to all.

This is interesting, because it could be seen as possibly clashing with respecting a person as an autonomous (self-determining) being which itself involves assisting the client in the 'pursuit of the actions and policies that he or she wishes to implement; or to try to remove personal, social or economic impediments to the realisation of their aspirations' (CCETSW 1976). Not very helpfully in terms of resolving possible conflict, Downie and Telfer describe social work as having to cope with the rights and duties of different social roles, so that the self-determination of clients as moral agents is maximized, and balanced against the rights of others within a liberal democracy.

'Personhood'
Central to any description of 'respect for persons', certainly within the framework of social work, is the definition of who and what

constitutes a person, or 'personhood'. The main question is, does 'person' apply to all categories of human beings? For example, does it apply to children, the senile, the mentally handicapped, the mentally ill, the ciminally insane etc.?

Noel Timms (1983, p. 61) comments that some commentators see 'respect for persons' as actively promoting discrimination against those who may not count as persons, or as being 'fully persons' according to what are agreed to be the criteria of 'personhood'. Downie and Telfer (1969, p. 35) provide a possible solution to this question of who to include as 'persons' by suggesting that 'respect' entails different emphases depending on the individual concerned. By their criteria, 'respect for persons' applied to rational individuals with full capabilities is the central case; particular individuals may approximate to this central case to a varying extent. Budgen (1982, p. 39) follows Downie and Telfer's argument through by suggesting that children can be seen as *potential* persons; the senile are *lapsed* persons; the mentally ill are *temporarily lapsed* persons; and the mentally handicapped can be considered to be *permanently potential* persons (!).

The important point is that according to Downie and Telfer (1969, p. 35) there are still sufficient resemblances between the above groups and fully 'rational' persons to justify including them in the principle of 'respect for persons'. A second aspect of their approach to 'persons' is to stress that there are possible attitudes (other than 'respect for persons') which are helpful in dealing with people in this 'minimal' sense. They suggest that affection and pity are relevant in dealing with this group of persons (as well as being relevant for dealing with fully rational persons). Whilst affection and pity in themselves are not moral attitudes, they are consistent with 'respect for persons' and can reinforce it. A final aspect of Downie and Telfer's solution to the problem of 'minimal' persons is that, all persons possess (equally) the characteristic of 'feeling', and as 'feeling' beings, all persons should be treated with 'respect for persons'.

Mentioned above was the fact that some commentators have been critical of 'respect for persons' because they see it as promoting discrimination against non-fully rational, or minimal persons. One such commentator is David Watson. Referring to 'minimal' persons, he writes that:

> a caring profession adopting this principle [respect for persons] must stigmatise individuals not exercising these [rational] capacities . . . the ability to choose for oneself etc. are hardly possessed by very young children and the senile, and not possessed

> at all by some severely mentally handicapped individuals; 'respect for persons' provides little or no moral reason, respectively, for the care of these individuals. We are only obliged to control them. Caring professions working with these individuals must find another principle if talk of 'caring' is to be taken seriously (Watson 1980, pp 59/60).

Watson's solution is to construct a principle of 'respect for human beings', on the grounds that this offers a wider range of characteristics than is included in 'respect for persons'. Watson comments that 'respect for human beings' could entail 'valuing the capacity to be emotionally secure, the desire to give and the capacity to receive love and affection, as well as the distinctive endowments of a human being' (1980, p. 61).

However, it is not at all clear just what Watson's replacement of 'persons' by 'human beings' actually introduces that could not be accommodated within 'respect for persons' itself. As Budgen states 'though "respect for persons" assumes choosers one can see it as capable of generalisation to the problem groups . . . such as the confused elderly' (1982, p. 40). The distinction which Watson makes between 'respect for persons' and 'respect for human beings' appears to be arbitrary. There is no logical disjunction (or at least not one explained by Watson) between the quality of, or needs of 'persons' and the quality of, or needs of 'human beings'. However, this does not actually constitute an argument against the criticism that non-fully rational 'persons' or 'human beings' are treated with less respect than fully rational persons. In fact, the later discussion of self-determination as positive freedom will suggest that within social work (which might be described as specializing in non-fully rational persons; or persons that society defines as such), such discrimination does exist.

Autonomy and paternalism

Obviously, the inclusion of 'minimal persons' in the principle of respect for persons has important implications for social work, not the least being the consideration of the relationship between autonomy or self-determination and paternalism. It can be plausibly argued that a principle of paternalism can be, or even needs to be developed which recognizes the need to intervene to protect the welfare and interests of 'minimal' persons.

Noel Timms (1983, p. 63), describes paternalism as involving:

> a turning of someone away from his current preferences or judgements; and the use of a particular kind of justification, generally

along the lines that the intervention was in the others' interest, or actually furthered his welfare.

Husak (1981) argues that a paternalistic relationship is necessarily built on a relationship of inferiority-superiority:

> Hence a lack of rationality, prudence, foresight, intelligence, maturity, or some other deficiency or shortcoming in which the alleged inferiority consists, seems necessary before paternalistic treatment could be thought appropriate.

As far as the principle of respect for persons in concerned, it is claimed that by acting in what are perceived to be the best interests of the client, the social worker is able to claim that he/she is operating within the conditions of the principle. However, in this form, it does appear that the individual's autonomy is potentially open to manipulation. It would also appear to be stretching the meaning and application of Kant's maxim that one should always respect the auto-nomy of *all* parties, since to do otherwise would mean that the maxim could not be 'willed to be universal law' in the appropriate sense. Interpreted in this strict way, the Kantian 'respect for persons' appears to be inconsistent with the concept of paternalism, since the latter necessarily requires some degree of manipulation. The apparent implausibility of Kant's principle which this argument highlights (in respect of its applicability to social work at least) can be illustrated by the following example.

If one saw a child standing at the kerbside, about to step into the road directly into the path of an approaching vehicle, one would have no hesitation in reaching out to stop the child in order to save him/her from serious, or perhaps fatal injury. By doing so one would be intervening paternalistically (by definition without the child's consent) in restricting the child's planned action (of stepping into the road); that is, one would be violating the child's autonomy. Strictly speaking, it might be argued that one would be violating the Kantian principle (given Downie and Telfer's inclusion of 'minimal' persons in the principle). However, by such an intervention, it could be rightly argued that by saving the child from injury (possibly fatal), one was in fact protecting the child's ability to remain a (potentially in the first instance, according to Downie and Telfer) rational, autonomous individual.

The important consideration here is that as individuals we exist through time and our long-term interests (for example not getting run over by large vehicles) may sometimes conflict with our short-term interests (for example crossing roads at particular points in time).

Certainly as far as the above illustration is concerned 'respect for persons' shóuld prescribe that one acts to promote a person's long-term interests, even at the expense of violating their autonomy or self-determination in the short term.

Richard Lindley (1984) in his discussion of strategic family therapy and 'respect for persons' suggests that more plausible than the strict interpretation of 'respect for persons' would be a more liberal interpretation which requires one to treat 'respect for persons' as a desirable goal, to allow for those situations when it may be necessary to violate a person's autonomy or self-determination.

However, the example of the child at the kerbside is relatively straightforward and uncontroversial in comparison with many examples that could be taken from social work practice, in which the justification for violating someone's autonomy or right to self-determination is not so straightforward. One such case might be that of deciding whether or not to 'accept' into residential care (against his/her own wishes) an elderly, confused person, judged to be incapable of caring for him/herself adequately, and also possibly to be in some way a danger to him/herself. Whilst it would appear that there are sufficient grounds to argue that such a person needs to be 'looked after' in order to protect their (future) interests (as perceived by others?) and self-determination, it is harder and more complex a matter to justify this violation of the person's immediate autonomy than it is to justify pulling the child back from the kerbside.

One of the differences between the child at the kerbside and the elderly confused person is that of assessing the degree and type of danger in both cases. The danger in the child's case is obvious, definite, and the immediate violation of the child's autonomy in order to protect the 'future' person is easily justified. But in the case of the confused elderly person, whilst the dangers involve in the person remaining at home are obvious, they are not necessarily imminent possibly may not even be realized, and the degree to which they threaten the well-being of the person needs to be assessed in terms of an estimation of the degree of risk involved, and in terms of the wishes of the person (i.e. to remain at home).

In their discussion of respect for persons, Clark with Asquith (1985, pp. 30/31) comment that rights or values derivative of 'respect for persons' (such as the right of self-determination) are qualified or limited, in that they may be denied in certain circumstances. For example,

(a) where the interests of others are adversely affected to an

unacceptable degree;
(b)   where there is a persistent wilful refusal to act morally;
(c)   where the person's actions break the law;
(d)   where the person's actions will damage his interests.

These qualifications and the discussion and illustrations above raise some important questions about 'respect for persons' as a social work value. This is especialy so in the context of the expectation of it as being the paramount social work value that describes the basis of the social worker's relationship with the client. The above discussion shows that this relationship is considerably more complex than is initially suggested in a simple statement of the value or ethic. Much of this complexity will become apparent in the discussion of self-determination in the next chapter.

2 Client Self-Determination

Within social work, self-determination (self-direction) has probably recieved more attention than any other value. Intuitively it is at the heart of what is generally considered to be one of the central tenets of social work:

> social workers should stimulate and enhance the client's capacity for making his own decisions and living his own life by his own standards. Social workers should not deceive or propel the client into a course of action that runs contrary to his true wishes (Clark with Asquith, 1985, p. 31).

Self-determination is seen first as an ethical principle, the breach of which negates the principle of 'respect for persons'; and also as a matter of 'common-sense', in that manipulative or coercive intervention is seen as not being effective in the long run. However, as was briefly indicated at the end of the last chapter, this principle or value is very difficult to understand in any absolute form.

Raymond Plant (1970, pp. 26-7) argues that social work moves away from the principle of 'respect for persons' when it begins to impose limits on, or violates client self-determination (the dilemma in the example at the end of the last chapter); and in so doing moves from a concept of 'negative freedom' to 'positive freedom'.

Basically, as it is characterized in most social work writing, self-determination contains these two aspects, 'negative freedom' and 'positive freedom' although, as Zofia Butrym comments, 'the paramount importance attached to the principle of self-determination in social work for most of its history is only matched by the degree of confusion regarding its nature' (Butrym, 1976, p. 54). Certainly, there are many different ways in which a complex concept such as self-determination may be defined and used (for example as can be seen in F.E. McDermott's 1975 collection of essays). However, as McDermott suggests (1975, p. 6) some of the confusion arises out of a failure to distinguish between the different versions of self-determination.

Negative freedom
Defined in its literal sense, which is the sense in which it is taken to be

a part of 'respect for persons', self-determination refers to 'that condition which an agent's behaviour emanates from his own wishes, choices and decisions' (McDermott, 1975, p. 3). In this sense, most human beings have a capacity for self-determination, and it is because of this that the term is not usually used as a description (because it does not actually add anything to a description of someone), but rather, it is generally used to 'express our commitment to it as a value'.

The most celebrated writer on the principle has been John Stuart Mill, particularly his essay 'On Liberty' (in Warnock, 1962) which is a powerful defence of the right to individual freedom. Mill argues that the state, or society at large (and its appointed agents), may only interfere with the freedom of individuals if it is to prevent them from doing harm to others. On this view it is wrong to coerce or manipulate a person simply to prevent him/her from harming him/herself or to prevent them from doing something which is considered morally wrong, but does not harm others. However, Mill does make special provision for children and others not capable of making 'rational' decisions by making them exceptions to his principle.

The traditional 'negative' exposition of self-determination as a social work value very much follows the literal definition as described by McDermott above. Biestek for example describes the principle as 'the practical recongnition of the right and need of clients to freedom in making their own choices and decisions in the casework process' (Biestek, 1961, p. 103).

Biestek goes on to say that one activity which is at variance with the principle is that of manipulation – that is the manoeuvering of the client:

> to choose or decide modes of action in accordance with the case-worker's judgement in such a way that the client is unaware of the process, or if he is aware of it, he feels 'moved about' against his will (1969, p. 107).

Zofia Butrym describes self-determination as a negative freedom as 'reflecting an individual's right to manage his own life and to make decisions concerning it' (1976, p. 52).

Similarly, Raymond Plant (who seems to draw heavily on the work of Isiah Berlin, 1969) describes negative freedom as encompassing 'non-interference', 'non-manipulation', and 'freedom from constraint'. Isiah Berlin himself describes negative freedom as 'freedom *from* [interference]' (1969, p. 131).

The reason why this analysis of freedom is characterized in philo-sophical thought as a 'negative' form of the concept of freedom is that its value and meaning lie in the desire to remove the obstacles in the way of one's exercising a capacity which one has. It also demands that others should refrain from coercing or imposing their will upon one. Ruth Wilkes goes further, and defines negative freedom in a more radical way when she says: 'negative freedom is freedom from inter-ference, the freedom to be what I am whether anyone likes it, or approves of it, or not' (Wilkes, 1981, p. 56).

The exercise of self-determination as negative freedom can be curtailed in many ways, most dramatically by imprisonment, but also by the imposition of legal penalties, by threats, and by various forms of psychological pressure and control. There is also a case referred to by McDermott (1975, p. 31) and by Ragg (1980, pp. 222-5) for extending the concept of freedom to cover controls on individual self-determination that arise from economic and social systems in so far as these are subject to human choice and control. For example, although a person may not be physically or legally prevented from obtaining adequate nourishment for him/herself, he/she may, because of his/her social position, be too poor to afford it. It could be argued that such poverty is just as much a curtailment of freedom (the freedom to obtain adequate nourishment) as might be any physical or legal restrictions.

Within social work, the dominant conception of the value of client self-determination is that of its being a condition of, or a means towards the development of the client. Florence Hollis sums this up very forcibly as follows:

> Why do we put all this stress on self-direction? Because we believe it is one of the greatest dynamics of the whole casework approach. Because we believe that the soundest growth comes from within . . . for this growth from within to occur there must be freedom to make mistakes as well as to act wisely (Hollis, 1967, p. 26).

The commitment to the value of self-determination in the promotion of client development clearly indicates that the client should be accorded freedom in the negative sense of the word. However, as McDermott (1975, p. 7) points out, whether the obligation to refrain from coercing or manipulating the client should be regarded as stemming from a fundamental right of the client as a rational human being (as according to 'respect for persons'), or merely as a pragmatic or technical principle for achieving certain social work goals is the point at which controversy breaks out. Certainly, though, it is apparent from the above quotations and explanation how the concept of negative freedom fits into and is central to Kant's 'respect for persons'. It is an essential part of the view of people as rational, autonomous, self-determining (within societal limits) individuals.

However, the actual place of 'negative freedom' in social work practice is not clear, and according to many commentators is non-existent. Martin Davies (1981, p. 84) sums up what seems to be a commonly held opinion about the principle of self-determination (as negative freedom) when he comments that recently, the principle has been exposed as something of a fraud: 'Both Plant and Whittington effectively killed off the concept as a pre-requisite of social work a decade ago, but the idea has remained a powerful fiction in the minds of practitioners' (Davies 1981, p. 84). Similarly, Helen Harris Perlman (in McDermott, 1975, p. 65) has described self-determination as '. . . nine-tenths illusion but one of the grand illusions.' However, as Timms has pointed out, the concept is not disposed of so easily. Its complexity and the difficulties it presents both theoretically and in its application are, suggests Timms, 'such that announcements of its demise may be counted as wish fulfillment' (Timms 1983, p. 54). Nevertheless the arguments against the principle's role and existence within social work are strong.

Whittington (in McDermott, 1975, pp. 81-92), for example, lists a number of ways in which the social worker limits client self-determination:

1 through the functions of her employing agency which might require her to use coercion or to have to employ statutory functions:
2 through the 'worker's power over clients' which stems from the worker's official (professional) power, for example, the power to decide whether or not to liaise on the client's behalf with the fuel boards when supply is threatened.
3 through the 'setting of the agency and the realities of time'. This refers to the institutional norms of the social worker's employing agency which the social worker has to conform to (to a greater or lesser degree) in order not to alienate herself, which in turn might reduce her ability to do the best for her client.
4 Whittington lists 'pressure and high caseloads', which limit the opportunity for the social worker to give time and encouragement, if not just recognize the client's right to self-determination.

Whittington also suggests that although the social worker may profess a commitment to client self-determination, non-directiveness and the client's right to choose, she may find her therapeutic aims greatly aided by the client's susceptibility to her 'influence and subtle directiveness.' Whittington concludes that:

> To increase the client's capacity to evaluate choices may be a goal of treatment, and participation may be a technique used to this end, but to maintain that treatment is carried out without directiveness because the latter's skilled and subtle nature has made it less easy to observe, requires nothing short of self-deception (Whittington in McDermott, 1975, p. 91).

In his summary of the views of Whittington and Alan Keith Lucas (in McDermott, 1975), who also criticize the role of self-determination in social work, McDermott make two points regarding their arguments. First, he says that the recognition of the right is incompatible with the authority and function that social workers are required to carry out. Second, to implement the right in practice would be unworkable, which, McDermott comments, implies that in so far as social work is working now, it is because the client's right to self-determination is accorded nothing more than 'lip-service'.

Positive freedom

Zofia Butrym, in discussing self-determination, suggests that over the last few decades the concept, has moved away from being an expression of 'negative freedom' to being an expression of 'positive freedom', which she describes as 'an extension of the range of choices available both within the personality and in the external environment' (Butrym 1976, p. 52).

According to Butrym, this move away from negative freedom has resulted in the social worker being more concerned with guiding the client towards more effective self-determination, in place of a concern for protecting the client's right to non-interference. This view is also held by McDermott, who says that:

> those who identify the concept of self-determination with that of positive freedom tend to play down its status as a right, and to emphasise its role as an ideal, or end to be pursued in the case-work process (McDermott, 1975, p. 7).

(It is interesting to note here that this view of self-determination has a utilitarian flavour, which contrasts with the Kantian base of self-determination as a negative freedom.) Another important consequence of this view is highlighted by Ruth Wilkes: 'The idea of positive freedom is concerned with the realisation of one's true self and justifies interference in the lives of others for their own good and for the good of society' (Wilkes, 1981, p. 57). Later on, Wilkes gives the warning: 'Coercion is usually recognised as a threat to freedom, but intervention in the life of another for their own good may be just as inimical to individual freedom.'

These are important points and will be considered in more detail later on, particularly with regard to how they relate to the concept of 'respect for persons'. First though, I will explain how and in what way it is argued that self-determination as positive freedom is justified.

Most human beings are capable of self-determination, although their capacity to exercise it rationally or constructively varies from individual to individual, and may also vary from time to time within each individual's life. From this it is possible to form an ideal of self-determination as positive freedom, on which one puts the highest possible value. Strictly speaking, this is to value self-determination not for itself (as characterized within respect for persons) but for the qualities, such as rationality, that characterize it in this ideal form. According to this 'idealist view', to be self-determining is to 'be liberated from the bonds of ignorance, prejudice and passion' (McDermott, 1975, p. 5).

It can also be seen as liberation in a socialist sense, from the crippling effects of a repressive and social system.

Of these interpretations of positive freedom, it is the idealist one that has dominated social work and so self-determination has come to be seen as something to be worked towards rather than as a basic right, which is the view of self-determination as negative freedom. By this view, whilst self-determination in the 'ordinary' (negative freedom) sense of the term is still considered as valuable in promoting the client's development, it tends to be subordinated to the view of self-determination as a positive freedom, which allows for the denial of the former right in the pursuit of the latter ideal.

In his essay 'Self-determination: king or citizen in the realm of values?' (in McDermott, 1975, pp. 34-42), Saul Bernstein places self-determination (which he initially uses in its literal, 'negative freedom' interpretation) in such a context. He begins his essay by asking the question 'Just how determining should self-determination be?' in order to examine whether self-determination (as 'negative freedom') should be the paramount ('king') social work value, or whether it should be regarded as just one form of or aspect of self-determination and social work values, the use and applicability of which is dependent on the particular situation and other considerations which might affect or modify the exercise of, and the ability to be self-determining.

The basis of Bernstein's argument is what he considers to be the 'supreme social work value' – 'human worth' – which he describes as 'based only moderately on what people are; much more on what they can be' (Bernstein in McDermott, p. 40). Legal and civil rights, standard of living, freedom to develop potentialities, intellectual and artistic interests are all important facets of this concept: 'As we study and diagnose each situation, our concern should be for maximising the choices for the people we serve . . . ' (Bernstein, p. 41). For Bernstein, the value of human worth – his supreme, or king of values – modifies self-determination, which whilst remaining 'supremely important' is not the supreme value: 'If what the client wants will result in the exploitation of others or the degradation of himself, the worker should try to help him change his desires' (Bernstein, p. 40). Bernstein discusses self-determination in stages of its complexity, (self-determination 1 – 6), starting with self-determination 1, which is its formulation in its basic, negative freedom sense, and ending with self-determination 6, in which he describes the value of human worth and the relationship of self-determination (in its basic sense) to it.

The complexities include: considerations about the dimension of time and the social worker's professional qualifications; that is, the difficulty which the social worker faces in assessing what the client wants and in helping him/her to achieve it, taking into account the varieties of ambivalence and changes over time. Also included are the effects of biological (health), economic and legal realities of self-determination, that is, that any exercise of self-determination which ignores such realities is 'unhealthy' and self-defeating. Closely related to this is the social dimension of self-determination: 'the complex network of social relationships which move the notion far from the simple level on which each client does what he wants to do, yields to his own impulse' (Bernstein, p. 37). This also involves protecting the client's legitimate self-determination where it is being violated. The complex process of decision making is also an important consideration in self-determination. For example, only as one takes account of all the relevant factors does true freedom operate in decision making. 'Yielding to unexamined impulses is more a surrender to instinctive drives than the expression of mature self-determination' (Bernstein, p. 39).

The discussion above indicates that the conception of self-determination as positive freedom is the one which in terms of role, aims and methods (whether 'statutorily' or 'professionally' determined) is dominant in social work. However, as was seen briefly through the quotations from Biestek and Wilkes, this conception of self-determination is open to the dangers of manipulation and coercion. Bernstein himself is aware of this when he writes that in addition to its values, the methods of social work also require stress on self-determination (in its literal sense): 'People can be and are manipulated, but constructive changes which take root inside the person, group, or community usually need to be based on participation and consent' (Berstein, p. 41).

Referring to the bulk of social work practice as having internal change as its goal, he argues that such a change is not achieved through imposing or giving orders, but by the active involvement of the client who comes to accept, on deepening levels, the process of change. He also argues that while social workers may 'enable, stimulate, impose, or even use force', what the client feels, thinks and ultimately values is his/her own private affair, and more within his/her control than that of the social worker.

However, Bernstein's argument here is not totally convincing and is at best only partial. To simply argue that in the end analysis, the individual's 'inner life' remains, or is something which is 'private' is questionable even if it could be tested in any way. But perhaps more important, Bernstein's defence avoids any questioning of the aims, goals and methods of social work itself which the criticisms of self-determination as positive freedom point towards.

One such criticism has come from Raymond Plant, who in referring to positive freedom writes:

Freedom conceived in this way may sanction influence and inter-ference in a person's life if it is likely to secure the goal of that person's self-realisation in the style of life toward which he is being influenced (Plant, 1970, p. 33).

As mentioned earlier, Plant's analysis leans heavily on Berlin's essay 'Two Concepts of Liberty', in which Berlin demonstrates how positive freedom evolved historically from a desire for self-mastery into a system of tyranny. Plant appears to fear a similar process within social work if the concept of self-determination is limited to 'positive freedom' and 'respect for persons' severely weakened.

Plant (1970, p. 27) quotes from Hollis's statement that: 'the client's right to self-determination exists until it is demonstrated that the exercise of this right would be highly detrimental to himself and to others. (From Hollis, 1940, pp. 5-6 *Social Casework in Practice).* Plant argues that if self-determination is a right, as it is according to the Kantian formulation of 'respect for persons', then it is difficult to see how its exercise can in any way be dependent on the social worker's assessment of the situation (implicit in Berstein's argument). He points out that there are groups of clients which have been regarded as being incapable of exercising the right to self-determination. For example, he cites L.C. Lane, who, referring to parents of difficult children, remarks that: 'the client frequently is not in a position to evaluate his problem by his own closeness to it . . . the helping person is outside the problem and can therefore see it more clearly.' (Lane, 'The Aggressive to Preventive Casework with Children's Problems' in *Social Casework*, vol. 33, Feb. 1952).

What concerns Plant here (and in examples from Hutchison and Perlman which he also cites) is that 'only certain things which the client chooses to do are to be counted as decisions' (Plant, 1970, p. 20). When a question arises about the ability of the client to be self-determining, the social worker becomes the authority:

> and this kind of view could sanction casework influence or even interference in these cases where a client is supposed not to have taken a real decision according to the criteria for decision making which are given by the casework theorists (Plant, 1970, p. 29).

For Plant it is very difficult to find any sort of knowledge which could justify such criteria. Once self-determination loses its status as a 'right' and becomes an ideal or goal, there is a danger of social work theory being used to manipulate and coerce people in the name of 'freedom': 'I am claiming that I know what they truly need better than they know it themselves. What, at most this entails, is that they would not resist me if they were so rational and as wise as I am, and understood their interests as I do' (Berlin, 1969, p. 133).

Another critic of the performance of positive freedom in social work has been Ruth Wilkes. She describes positive freedom as 'concerned with the realization of one's true self and justifies interference in the life of others for their own good and the good of society' (Wilkes, 1981, p. 57). Wilkes argues that intervention in another person's life can be just as great a threat to their freedom (self-determination) as coercion is recognized as being. She argues that the wish to be in charge of one's own life may lead 'high-minded persons' (social worker?) to think that they must make it as easy as possible for the individual to realize his/her 'true' self and master his/her 'bad' self. It is easy, she argues, for society/social workers to convince themselves that for the good of other people, individuals (clients) must be given insight into what they really want or really are (as opposed to what they actually want or think are). Once this is done, knowledge of their expressed wishes is assumed and they are helped to realize their true potential by 'well known techniques of management and manipulation'. And so, the individual or client becomes her 'best or most reasonable self', and 'the empirical matter-of-fact self is strictly controlled'.

Very interestingly, Wilkes (p. 58) provides two contrasting lists of what she sees as the distinguishing features of negative freedom and positive freedom, which includes:

NEGATIVE FREEDOM (empiricist)	POSITIVE FREEDOM (rationalist)
Main features:	
Empirical and unsystematic	Speculative and rationalistic
Spontaneous and little understood	Utopian
Inarticulate	Plausible
Assumptions:	
Essence of freedom is spontaneity and lack of coercion	Freedom is realized in attainment of a collective purpose
Method is trial and error	Method is enforcement of pattern
Cannot do good, can only avoid evil	Can make man workable
There is an essential human nature	Human nature is mouldable
Man is fallible and sinful	Man is naturally intelligent and good

It is possible to see from the two lists that whilst Wilkes puts the argument in a wide philosophical context (almost mystical at times), she basically agrees with Plant, in that through the adoption of self-determination as positive freedom, the rights of the individual have been superseded to a great extent by the externally determined 'ideal' of the person.

Whilst she accepts that social workers accept the value of the individual as an end in him/herself, once the emphasis is on conscious planned change (as in self-determination as positive freedom), it is 'not possible to stand back and let things be': 'Activities are goal orientated, task-centred, and purposeful, and social work intervention, more often than not, is based on approval in terms of what is socially acceptable' (Wilkes, 1981, p. 59).

Wilkes's argument goes significantly beyond Plant's criticism of positive freedom when she describes how the idea and assumptions of positive freedom have come to dominate and reflect the kind of society in which we live. The assumptions of positive freedom are, she argues, very much taken for granted, whereas the word 'negative' has come to be associated with derogatory implications in contemporary thinking, because it runs contrary to our problem solving way of looking at the world. When the idea that the individual (client) can be improved by someone else (social workers) is linked to the idea that values are man-made, the result is, she says, a 'recipe for disaster': 'It is dangerous because of the absence of moral values and because of the authority it gives to experts to impose their views of others' (Wilkes, 1981, p. 59).

Here she is referring to a view of people based on the assumption that we create ourselves, and that there is no 'substantial self', and thus we are able to mould and control people. Human nature is essentially something which is culturally determined and open to change by human behaviour. An alternative view (which Wilkes argues for), is that human nature is a part of 'basic reality' and it does not change with different circumstances, and is essentially the same everywhere. The implications of these two 'world views' are that, by the first concept of human kind it is 'possible to discriminate between human beings by concentrating on those [or parts of . . .] who are amenable to improvement by various methods' (1981, p. 61). Thus, she argues that the old, the senile, the sick, the dying, severely handicapped people (all minimal persons?) are a low priority because they are not amenable to change. According to the second 'world view', a person's dignity is not related to any personal attributes such as 'virtue, youth, or social value', but to that which is inherent in every person, and so: 'love of one's neighbour applies to all, by virtue of one's common humanity, and no exceptions are permitted' (1981, p. 61).

Running through Wilkes's argument is the need for a morality or ethic which transcends the 'material' life of 'humankind', in the way that the Kantian 'respect for persons' is universal and a measure by which we can evaluate our goals and actions as being moral or not.

3 Conclusions

Clearly emerging from the discussion of respect for persons and self-determination are many difficulties and complexities of argument. This is so in at least three ways.

First, from a philosophical standpoint many of the issues and questions raised by these concepts remain substantially unresolved amongst philosophers themselves.

Second, and closely related to the first point as far as their application to social work is concerned, it is obvious that once one goes beyond simply stating what the values are, their actual meaning is unclear and at times ambiguous, especially in the context of their role as guidelines for practice.

Third, in the context of social work practice, from the questions and criticisms raised (for example by Whittington and Plant) it appears that the relevance of and use of these values within practice is unclear and questionable.

The task here is not to attempt to resolve the philosophical implications and problems raised. It would, however, be useful at this stage to attempt to place the discussion in a moral philosophical context in as much as this may help to clarify the issues as they relate to social work practice. This can be done by looking at respect for persons and self-determination as negative freedom; and self-determination as positive freedom in the context of deontological and utilitarian ethics, respectively. Whilst both 'ethics' have initial appeal, they also suffer from serious weakness in the context of being guides for making ethical decisions, which is particularly relevant to social work.

Respect for persons (including self-determination as negative freedom) belongs to the deontological 'camp', in which certain actions are inherently right or good, or right or good as a matter of principle, and thus ought to be engaged in. In this sense, and as was argued by Ruth Wilkes, self-determination should be right. The problem, however, with this approach is that it fails to provide the necessary guidelines for resolving conflicts of opinion or duty. This relates specifically to social work in that, as was mentioned in the Introduction, social work is reluctant to face possible conflicts in its "value talk', or relate its ethics to conflicts (or possible conflicts) of opinion and expectations in social work practice. This is particularly evident within BASW's *Code of Ethics.*

The utilitarian approach argues that actions ought to be performed, or beliefs held, not because they are intrinsically good, but because they are 'good' by virtue of their consequences. Within the context of social work, the value of self-determination as positive freedom lies not so much in its inherent worth as 'a right', but in view of the consequences or benefits of being self-determining. In other words, self-determination is instrumental to the 'ideal' functioning of the individual rather than expressive of some ultimate conviction as it is in its negative form in respect for persons.

However (as Reamer, 1982, points out), there are dangers and problems within utilitarian ethics. First, utilitarians have not yet determined how consequences that are qualitative in nature can in fact be quantified. How and by what criteria can the 'good' of self-determination be quantified? Second, they have not solved the problem that the rights of a few can be subordinated for a presumably greater good. That is, the 'rights' of an individual or individuals could be denied or manipulated to conform to the 'ideal' or greater good of others (the majority?). As was seen in the arguments of Plant and Wilkes, this is precisely what makes the advocates of negative freedom suspicious because it opens the door for manipulative or repressive actions and policies.

The distinctions between deontological and utilitarian ethics are important to consider because actions and policies implemented on these bases will often have substantially different aspects. Also they offer a means of understanding and explaining some of the apparent 'value' ambiguities within social work practice.

By asserting the value and rights of each individual person, respect for persons (and self-determination as negative freedom) is deontological in its nature. This is, however, in contrast to the utilitarian aim of promoting the common good, which Clarke with Asquith (1985) and Davies (1981), for example, suggest is the function of social work. As such, social work depends primarily on the concept of 'positive' freedom, which expands the area of what can be considered to be 'justifiable paternalism'.

According to this view, the function of social work is seen as an activity which promotes the resources and opportunities considered necessary for a decent or 'good life', and which involves taking a wide range of welfare responsibilities, 'even when the intended beneficiaries have not sought help' (Clarke with Asquith, 1985, p. 62). To have a need implies lacking a 'good' whose possession is, in an important way conducive to happiness (or acceptability). From this, the task of social work can be seen as an attempt to maximize the well-being of individuals and that of the community as a whole.

Clarke with Asquith comment that 'social work is not merely a service to be provided in a neutral or passive manner for those who choose to make use of the kind of help it can offer' (1985, p. 62). Very brief though this analysis is at this stage, it does offer a means of understanding the nature of some of the 'value' problems and conflicts within social work. The social worker essentially is caught between a deontologically based set of 'professional' ethics, and a utilitarian-based practice 'reality'. In local authority social work, the agency has a responsibility to ('the good') society as well as the individual, and the social worker employed in the agency therefore has a responsibility to represent society's interests, expectations and ideals, as well as the 'rights' of the individual.

In this context, social work's code of ethics does not appear to offer the social worker any clear resolution of the moral issues that arise out of this situation of potentially conflicting demands. Statements such as: 'Members of a profession have obligations to their clients, to their employers, to each other, to colleagues in other disciplines, and to society' (BASW, 1975) offer no guidance to the social worker precisely at the point where dilemmas specific to social work practice arise.

Related to this criticism, and also offering an explanation of the failure of social work values to relate to social work practice, is Pearson's argument that:

> while the social work ethic gives a more elaborate account of client *rights*, it gives only the poorest indication of the other side of the equation, (i.e. that client rights are limited): the social worker's ethic in theory offers a limitless relationship, although in practice, of course, the social worker is able to offer no such thing. For the social worker is an official of a bureaucratic organisation, as well as a person engaged in a 'relationship' (Pearson, 1975, pp. 50/51).

Two important points emerge at this stage. First, traditionally, 'value-talk' in social work tends to concentrate solely on the relationship between the social worker and client. Second, social work, as suggested in the previous argument, is practised within (local authority) organizations, the demands of which necessarily affect the way in which social work values 'work'. Pearson illustrates this by listing two sets of values. First of all he gives a 'traditional' list of values (1975, p. 50), and then he gives a 'hidden' list of values which takes account of the organizations/bureaucracy in which most social workers are employed, and the 'realities' of social work practice

Traditional list:

1 The client has a right to expect that his communications should have a confidential status.
2 The client has the right to determine the course of his own actions [the principle of self-determination].
3 The client has the right not to be judged by the social worker [the 'non-judgemental' attitude].
4 The client should be regarded with warmth and positive feelings, whatever his actions [the notion of 'acceptance'].
5 Underlying all these is a general principle of 'individuation', each man is unique; all men have innate dignity and worth (Pearson, 1975, p. 50).

'Hidden' list:

1 The client's communications to officials of a public service, involving as they do matters of public money, and in the last analysis public order, have the character of public knowledge.
2 The client's actions, impinging on the rights of others and on the obligations and priorities of public service, are not free.
3 The client's actions, by their nature problematic to 'consensus', are judged.
4 The client's rights as a citizen do not entitle him to anticipate that regardless of any act on his part he will continue to be 'accepted': he can, in short, be 'outlawed'.
5 Clients, as the objects of a large-scale organisation with many bureaucratic features, will be treated within an administrative machinery as 'cyphers' (1975, p. 53).

The ambiguities, compromises and obvious infringements of the 'traditional' list. Pearson argues, cannot be simply dismissed as bad social work practice. They represent society's, and the social work agency's demands and expectations of the social worker, and the 'bureaucratic' nature of the agency: 'if social work is anything, it is an organisationally grounded practice, and social work's ethic is but one side of an incomplete equation' (Pearson, 1975, p. 51).

It is a failing of much that has been written on and about social work values that it has concentrated solely on the relationship between the social worker and individual/client. Where reference is made to the context in which this relationship takes place it is mostly secondary to the relationship itself and offers no more than a vague or general reference which avoids examination of possible conflicts of values. The quotations from BASW (p. 11), CCETSW (p. 14) and the argument from Downie and Telfer (p. 14) illustrate this point.

Yet from the discussions above, of deontological and utilitarian moralities and Pearson's argument, it seems obvious that in order to examine and understand what social work values are, and how they 'work' in practice, the context in which they are practised has to be given equal consideration. That such things as society's expectations and norms, and agency demands and functions are important in understanding social work values has been indicated in this chapter: both in the sense of possible conflicts between different moral philosophies and in the sense that their effect on social work values is largely unexamined. In order to examine these issues further and in greater detail it is first necessary to look specifically at what does happen to values in practice.

PART II
VALUES IN PRACTICE

Part II is a direct response to the questions arising out of, and the arguments begun in Part I, in that it consists of a small-scale empirical/conceptual study of 'what happens' to values in local authority-based social work practice. The general aim of the study was to observe and analyse values in this context, in which, as was suggested in the Conclusions to Part I, the exercise and relevance of 'respect for persons' and client self-determination (as both negative and positive freedom) is by no means as clear or unproblematical as much of the theory and literature on social work values suggests.

4 Methodology

Aims

The aim of the study was to find out and examine how social work values (concentrating on respect for persons and client self-determination) 'work' in social work practice. In particular, I was interested in the extent to which social work values in the relationship between social worker and client are affected, compromised or determined by 'outside' factors such as agency function, and expectations from other professionals, groups or individuals.

Method

The study was conducted by interviewing individual local authority social workers who described a particular case that they were currently involved with, or had been involved with very recently. This was to avoid general statements about what values social workers thought were or were not important or relevant, and also to avoid simply compiling a general list of considerations or constraints regarding values in practice. By basing the study on specific current or very recent cases it was hoped to be able to identify and examine in detail how social work values actually (rather than 'might' or 'should') work in practice. I was also aware that different types of cases might determine and illustrate different ways in which values work in practice.

The cases

Apart from active or recent involvement, the other main criterion regarding the type of cases that I wanted to study was that they should preferably involve some stage at which the social worker was involved in decision making, either on his/her own, or with other 'professionals', agencies, or interested individuals or groups. This was because I thought that the decision-making process might highlight and illustrate the values and value choices to be made, and also other factors that had to be considered in the decisions to be made.

The two most important criteria for selecting the cases to be studied were those outlined above. The specific nature of the case, i.e. whether child care, statutory, admission to care etc. was secondary. However, when contacting the social workers who agreed to describe one of their cases, I did suggest particular types of cases, mainly on the bases that they would probably fit the main criteria, but also because I did not want to end up with all the same types of case. Although this would have been an interesting exercise in its own right, I was more interested in examining how values work in different contexts than in making a comparison of different social workers' handling of the same type of case.

Altogether six interviews were conducted. This number was determined by the relatively short time available in which to complete this part of the original thesis and the time it took to analyse in depth the cases themselves, rather than a deliberate intention to interview a specific number of social workers.

Negotiating the study
The six social workers interviewed worked in three separate area teams. Initial contact was made with their area officers to whom the aims and methods of the study were explained, and assurances given regarding the use of any material from the interviews. The original choice of officers to approach was made on the basis of those whom it was considered would be most likely to agree to help, and from whom permission to approach 'their' social workers could be gained 'informally', so as to save time negotiating through formal/bureaucratic channels which would have taken much longer. The area officers then suggested social workers whom they thought would be willing to be interviewed. All the social workers contacted agreed to help, and arrangements were made to meet and interview them.

The interviews
The interviews lasted between one and one-and-a-half hours, which was the length of time that I considered reasonable to request from the interviewees. Rather than take notes, which would have been distracting to myself and the interviewees, the interviews were tape-recorded which made it possible to concentrate wholly on what was being said. Having a complete record of the interviews also made the later analysis more thorough.

In the interviews, the interviewees were asked to relate the 'story' of the case, that is, describe the sequence of events, and the nature of their involvement, from which I concentrated on what I considered to be the important events and decisions in the light of my aims, and I questioned the interviewees further on these. I did not impose any structure or predetermined set of questions on the interviewees, but did have a set of general 'headings' or 'clues' to which reference could be made during the interviews. These were:

Assumptions   Whose? Why?
Presumptions   What? Whose?

Decisions	What? Whose? Who with? Why?
Standards	Whose?
Whose values?	social worker's
	social work agencies'
	other professionals'
	client's
	society's
What was the social worker's job/strategy?	

This list of 'clues' was intended to focus my listening and questioning of the cases to enable me to identify what values were relevant to the case, and how they were working.

Comments on the study
All the interviewees proved to be cooperative and interested in describing their cases. They differed though in the degree to which they were able to reflect on some aspects of their cases, for example in analysing why certain decisions or actions were important at a particular time, In some of the cases there seemed to be situations in which the following of 'accepted practice' or 'official procedure' completely disguised the 'value content' of the decisions and actions being taken. (However, it would be fair to take into account my own interviewing skills – or lack of them – in considering this comment.

Related to this is a further observation on the interviews that the task of focusing on the decision-making process was not as easy or clear as initially anticipated. On occasions, the point at which decisions were actually made, and the decision-making process itself, were difficult to recognize, for example by the social worker following the 'accepted practice' in certain situations, or by 'official/ statutory procedures' which may have removed from the social worker some of the need and (individual) decision-making responsibility. Also, it was apparent in some of the cases that the social worker was not necessarily the person involved in the case with the central decision-making authority or power. These points will be illustrated in the description of the cases themselves.

Obviously, the scale of the study is only exploratory in terms of the numbers of interviews conducted and the different types of cases examined, which necessarily determines and limits quantitatively the use to which the findings and conclusions can be put. It would, for example, be illegitimate to draw any conclusive or 'universally applicable' conclusions about how social work values operate in specific types of cases from the study. However, I think that the cases are *illustrative* in a general sense of the way in which values are affected and determined in practice by other considerations/factors, and specific to the cases described in detail, illustrate in depth social work values at work.

5 The Client/Social Worker Relationship is only Half of the Story . . .

In this chapter I will briefly describe how, in all six cases, the role and place of the values of respect for persons and client self-determination were influenced and compromised. The 'value qualifications' came from or were imposed by individuals, agencies, bureaucratic demands and statutory requirements which influenced and determined the nature of the social worker/client relationship, and hence the way in which the values worked within this relationship. I have included the social worker's statutory responsibilities in this, for clarification purposes, although it can be rightly argued that in the context of local authority-based social work, such responsibilities, where they are present, are central to the social worker's relationship with the client.

The six cases were as follows:

A The admission of an elderly, confused lady to Part III accommodation against her wishes.
B A referral from a husband regarding his wife who was suffering from depression, and which led to family therapy.
C A social worker mediating between client and Housing Department in order to get council accommodation for the client following eviction for substantial rent arrears.
D A specialist mental handicap social worker's management of an 'independent living' group home for three mentally handicapped adults, and the contrary bureaucratic restraints placed on his habilitation work at the home.
E The voluntary admission of an adolescent girl to care who had been rejected by her mother, and was a persistent school refuser.
F The supervision of a two-year-old child on the 'At risk' register.

'Value qualifications'

1 From other agencies/professionals/individuals - applied to cases A, B and C
In case A, the elderly lady (Mrs M)'s GP, the home help organizer, and in the end, officials from the gas board all played a part in the eventual denial of her right to self-determination. Concern about her

ability to live at home expressed by her neighbours and family also challenged Mrs M's right to be self-determining. The result of this 'pressure' was that Mrs M's right to be self-determining was seen and judged by the social worker in the context of the perspectives of these individuals (professional and non-professional), more so than it was in accordance with Mrs M's own wishes.

In case B, concern and pressure from the GP regarding the wife's mental health influenced the degree of pressure that the social worker put on her and her family to continue with family therapy sessions, even though she and two members of her family did not wish to continue. Their right to make their own decisions, to determine their involvement in the sessions, was thereby compromised.

In case C, the legal authority of the Housing Department determined the nature of the social worker's relationship with the client, and initially determined the client's ability (or lack of it) to be self-determining, by denying her the right to council accommodation.

2 Statutory requirements and responsibility applied to cases A, E and F

In all three cases these crystallized the social worker's responsibility for the demands and values of their employing agencies and society's expectations, which were not always in accord with 'social work values' in the context of the client/social worker relationship. This was so in case A in which the client's right to self-determination was eventually seen in the context of the criteria for its denial laid down in Section 47 of the National Assistance Act 1948, and which was finally used to deny her the 'right' of self-determination.

In case E, although the admission to care was voluntary, once the adolescent had been admitted, the social worker's responsibility for her welfare restricted the degree of self-determination that she could be allowed, even though the social worker herself felt that at times this was not in her client's best interests. In case F, the nature and demands of the Supervision Order determined and defined the relationship between the social worker and the family.

3 Restraints/limitations from own agency

In case D, this was particularly pronounced, in that relationship with the members of the group home which their ability to be self-determining could g the administrative/bureaucratic demands of the department. That is, they insisted that they shou the resident's pension and supplementary benefit the opportunity and the extent to which the res budget and take responsibility for their financial affairs, which in turn limited their ability to become self-determining.

Obviously, this is only a very bare sketch of the cases and the value considerations in them. However, it does indicate that in understanding how values work in social work practice, one must take account of the social worker's responsibilities as defined (or limited) by the employing agency, and the expectations, rights, and demands of others (professional and non-professional). The nature of the social work task in each case determines the nature of the social worker's relationship with the client. In other words, the social worker/client relationship as it is sometimes discussed (particularly in the 'value' literature), as if it were independent of and separate from the context and reasons for the relationship coming about in the first place, is inadequate for understanding the place of the social work values within this relationship. The relationship itself in its 'ideal' or 'casework' form is only half of the story in understanding how values work in practice. The context in which the relationship takes place is equally important, as in reality this determines the nature of the relationship and the way in which the values of respect for persons and self-determination operate within the relationship.

The next two chapters are an attempt to illustrate this argument, through a detailed examination and analysis of two of the cases outlined above, case A and case C. I have chosen these two cases because the social workers concerned with them were the most forthcoming and open in describing them to me, and also because each case is very different from the other. Together they illustrate different expectations, responsibilities and roles of the social workers involved, and hence different ways in which 'values' are used and work.

Obviously in the descriptions and analysis of the cases the names of the people involved have been changed to protect their confidentiality, and the social worker in each case is referred to as 'SW', although it should be remembered that the social worker in each case is different. In the descriptions of the cases themselves I have, as far as possible, used quotations from the social workers in order to give as full and accurate a description as possible of how they described their cases to me.

6 Case A: Mrs M – Description and Analysis

Description

Client self-determination – a right?

This first case concerns Mrs M, aged 94 years, who lived on her own in a rather neglected, large detached house. She has a son (who works in Saudi Arabia), and two daughters, Mary and Maureen. Mary has recently had cancer and visits her mother occasionally (but regularly), and Maureen visits twice a week, sometimes more. Mrs M was first referred to the social services in 1982 by her daughter Maureen, who said that her mother was finding it increasingly difficult to look after herself properly, despite her (Maureen's) regular visits. She also said that 'the job was getting her down and she never received any thanks or acknowledgement from her mother for the things that she did for her'.

A social worker (SW), visited Mrs M, finding the house to be 'smelly and tatty', and described Mrs M as 'a forthright and domineering old lady,' and she 'refused to accept any help from us. She told me all the help she wanted was someone to do up her buttons because she had severe arthritis'. Her arthritis meant that Mrs M was often unable to dress herself properly, and that she frequently dropped things. SW also described Mrs M as having poor eyesight and as being forgetful. For example, she would turn on the gas and forget to light it:

> She was also smelling and it was fairly obvious, although she would never let me go look in her bedroom, that she was probably sleeping in a wet bed and wet sheets, except for when her daughter [Maureen] came round and actually changed the bed for her.

Following SW's visit, the home help organizer visited Mrs M (on the suggestion of SW) and her help was also refused. Over the next year SW visited several times a week to:

> maintain contact . . . . with my style of social work, when I go see somebody like Mrs M, and they resist offers of help. I don't simply close their case and go away until the inevitable crisis occurs. I feel it's important if possible to form a relationship with them of some sort so that eventually when they do have to move, they are not

totally alone, but that they have got some sort of warmth and someone that they can trust.

However, Mrs M still refused any help, and the case was closed.

> We were getting nowhere, and then we re-opened it when her daughter [Maureen] again asked for help. It was the same reasons that the daughter was saying that she couldn't go on with the level of help that was needed, and she was getting so little reward from her mother for all that she was doing . . . . The pressure was beginning to tell on her and she in fact was going to the doctor with a bad back which was probably due to the tension and strain of it all.

Soon after Mrs M accepted a home help and the incontinent laundry services were started, 'so the situation had got pretty bad.' Following this 'the daughter found the situation improved and the case was then made non-active.'

In late 1983, Maureen again visited SW and said that she and Mary were going to try and persuade their mother to accept permanent residential care in the new year. SW visited Mrs M in January 1984 and found that her situation had deteriorated:

> Mrs M's faculties are fading, and it seems to me that she is at risk. I felt very much that Mrs M could no longer cope living alone, and I talked to her about considering some sort of change, so that I was quite keen for her to go for some short-term care so that she could get some idea of what a residential home was like . . . . often she would get up at 6 a.m. and light the fire before the home help got there, and she would sit very close to the fire, and she would put things like wet knickers to dry very close to the fire, so that it was a danger. I was also very aware that she was not feeding herself properly. She would talk to me about having quite nutritious meals, but when I discussed it with the home help, you could see from her wastebin that she was probably living on bread and butter and hot drinks, and her 'Sanatogen' – her favourite tipple.

SW persuaded Mrs M to visit a private residential home for the elderly with her and also a social services run home, and although Mrs M said that she liked the social services home, she stoutly refused to go there as a resident, even for a 'short break'.

At the end of February, the daughter Mary told SW that both she and Maureen were getting fed up and she felt that they would not be able to cope much longer. Maureen was now seeing her doctor 'for her nerves'. SW went to see the GP (the same for Mrs M and her daughters), and they agreed that she (SW) would try to persuade Mrs M to go into the social services run home (which Mrs M had previously visited and liked), while Maureen went on holiday. Mrs M agreed to go to the home for two weeks over Easter, and it was arranged by SW that the home could provide a permanent bed for her should 'there be any chance that she might agree to stay there.' However, a few hours after her admission (at which she seemed quite happy), SW had a phone call from the home saying that 'Mrs M was creating mayhem and they couldn't cope with her any longer, so please would I take her home?' SW went to the home and tried to reason with Mrs M but was unsuccessful: 'She said that if I didn't take her home, she'd hail a lorry. She's 94 don't forget.'

So Mrs M returned home and SW arranged extra home help visits over the Easter holidays while Maureen was away. Immediately after the Easter holiday, SW received a letter from Mary saying that she was not going to visit any more, 'she just couldn't go on any longer with it.'

Meanwhile Mrs M was behaving very obstructively towards the home help, refusing to let her change her bed and on one occasion she 'raised her walking stick to her.'

When the GP talked to her about her selfishness she said she wanted to change her GP. At this point we discussed the possibility of a Section 47 [of the 1948 National Assistance Act], but agreed that there were not yet grounds for this. But if the family stayed clear as they were saying they would, the situation would soon come to it. [The criteria for using the Act are listed on p. 58-9].

On SW's next visit, she found Mrs M to be 'happy as a sandboy', looking forward to the return of Maureen from holiday. However, despite the extra home help hours that Mrs M had been receiving, she described her 'condition' as deteriorating:

There were faeces on the floor and the bed was wet every night . . . she always sat in the same chair, and that was very well awash. She has an open fire in her oak-pannelled sitting room where she sat all the time, and there was a considerable risk with this I thought.

Between May and July the situation remained much the same. An attempt was made by SW to get Mrs M to go for day care in the hope that this would lessen some of the pressure on her daughters, mainly Maureen, and also provide practical support for Mrs M during the day. Mrs M tried it for two days but then refused to go any more. At the end of June Maureen had a 'violent argument with her mother and told SW that she would no longer continue to visit her mother.'

At the beginning of July SW received a letter from the home help organizer saying that Mrs M was leaving the gas on unlit, and that she was claiming that the home helps had stolen spoons, forks and silver from the house. On a later investigation of blocked drains it was found that Mrs M had flushed them down the toilet. SW also received a letter from the Gas Board expressing concern at the risk of the gas being left on, and saying that they felt that the gas should be disconnected. Once again SW and the GP considered using Section 47 of the National Assistance Act 1948 after the gas board threat to disconnect, but once again decided that they did not have sufficient grounds to do so (I will discuss this in further detail later on:) 'So it is a very complex case of somebody who in many ways is becoming senile, but is extremely cleverly manipulating the situation.'

On SW's next visit, Mrs M agreed to accept meals on wheels, but the day after they had started SW received a note from the meals on wheels organizer saying that Mrs M had told them not to call again. At about this time Mrs M began telephoning her son-in-law at work, up to a dozen times a day, which was 'causing him considerable difficulties at work . . . . She usually rang to ask him to do things for her such as replace her kettle, which she regularly burnt out by switching it on without putting any water in it.'

At the end of July, Mrs M became ill with a urinary infection for which her GP prescribed a course of antibiotics which, he suspected, she was not taking. At the end of August Mrs M made further allegations that her spoons and silver were being taken: 'I found it impossible to reason with her.'

At the same time British Telecom contacted SW to inform her that they were going to charge Mrs M £28 each time they had to reconnect her telephone. Apparently when she could not get through to someone she was ringing, she became angry and 'pulled the wire out of the wall'. She also started to complain to the police that her daughters were refusing to visit her: 'If she wanted to stir things up with the family she'd say that nobody had been near her.'

In September, Mrs M spoke to SW about 'going into a home for the winter', and SW took her to visit a private home, which she said she would be willing to go into in December. But unknown to SW, she had advertised in the local paper 'a room to let for a student', which contradicted her intention to accept residential accommodation. Mrs M did not 'let' a room and refused to discuss going into residential accomodation.

At the beginning of October SW received a note from the home help saying that she had had to climb into the house through an open window on her last visit because Mrs M could not get the door unlocked. By now there was no contact at all between Mrs M and her daughter Maureen:

> Mrs M would say things to me like, 'the daughter's a devil', and 'I never want to see her again'. In fact the daughter was extremely upset and said that by visiting her mother she was only making herself ill and was not helping the situation at all. I agreed with her.

Two days later:

> . . . . things came to head because when the home help arrived there was a strong smell of gas and the home help found that Mrs M had jammed the gas tap full on, and she tried to stop the home help phoning for help, and insisted on returning to the kitchen to light the gas. The home help had to forcibly remove the matches from her, and the home help phoned the office. By this time Mrs M had found more matches and wanted to go back to the kitchen, but 'they' got the gas board out and the home help got Mrs M to the garden, with difficulty. The gas board arrived and cut off the gas, so Mrs M had no means of cooking. [She was also still refusing to have meals on wheels.] On the following day I had a meeting at the house with the community physician and the GP. Mrs M had, the previous night, attempted to heat up water in a saucepan on the open fire, and on the visit with the community physician and the GP, she agreed to go into our home at — where there was the only vacancy.

In explaining why it was at this time that the community physician was involved, SW commented: 'I felt that the point was reached when she could no longer manage on her own, and in the circumstances there was no other help we could give her to enable her to stay at home'. Both the community physician and the GP agreed that Mrs M could not remain at home.

> . . . and the community physician who is always extremely reluctant, thank goodness, to make orders, said that in his opinion an order would be granted, but if there was any chance she would go 'in' voluntarily, we should try that first. But if she went in to the home and did as she had done previously, and demanded to be taken home again, then he would invoke the order. So it was that near, and the GP absolutlely agreed with this.

'On the one hand I will support someboby's right to independence to the hilt, but . . . '

I would now like to look in greater detail at the role played by SW, by illustrating from the interview how her relationship with Mrs M (and the subsequent action taken) developed, and the extent to which it was influenced by the interest and concern of Mrs M's family, SW's consideration of the community in which Mrs M lived, her GP, and the adequacy of the domiciliary/community-based services that she received. I will also illustrate what SW's own thoughts and feelings were during her involvement in the case.

Family. Consideration of Mrs M's family was (increasingly as the case progressed) an important factor in SW's intervention in the life of Mrs M. The initial and second referrals both came from Mrs M's daughter, Maureen. Also, as the case progressed, both daughters complained to SW of the mental and physical strain that they were under in caring for their mother. This pressure from the family increased as Mrs M's faculties decreased and also as Maureen and Mary's relationship with their mother deteriorated, to the point eventually where contact between them and their mother ceased altogether. The family's practical support of their mother also became an important consideration in whether or not Mrs M was able to, or should remain at home: 'we [SW and the GP] discussed the possibility of a Section 47, but agreed that there were not yet grounds for this, but if the family stayed clear, the situation would soon come to it.'

SW was sympathetic to the plight of Maureen and Mary, and her consideration of their plight played a significant part in her decision to:

1 persuade Mrs M to accept domiciliary support;
2 attempt to persuade Mrs M to accept short-term care whilst Maureen went on holiday;
3 persuade and eventually force Mrs M to accept permanent residential care, which originally was the family's decision.

In explaining her reasoning and motives behind these decisions and her eventual considerations about the applicability of Section 47 of the National Assistance Act 1948, SW said:

Yes, there's various factors. There's the family who were extremely upset, and the daughter who stopped visiting was on the verge of a breakdown about the whole thing – it had really got her down. I was obviously very aware of the anguish of her family and that must have come into my reasoning.

A small, but specific example of SW's awareness of, and receptivity to the 'family's anguish' can be seen in the quotation below, which is the response to a question I asked about whether in July when the Gas Board first expressed concern, SW considered any alternative means of cooking:

> No, we talked this over with the family – what about getting her an electric cooker? They begged me not to consider an electric cooker. She had had electric cookers in the past and simply either turned them on and left them on, or turned the plates on until they were red hot, and then put the tea towels to dry on them. The risk as just as great – it seemed to me that there was no alternative.

Neighbours/community. Another important consideration for SW in the case were the interests of Mrs M's neighbours and local community:

> she was also a great nuisance to the neighbours. She was forever ringing and asking them to do things for her, and she was also using the 'Good Neighbour Scheme' beyond what was reasonable. She would ask them to take her into the city to buy some tea and then be unable to get into the shop to do it . . .

When I asked how important her demands on and her relationship with her neighbours were in assessing Mrs M's 'fitness' to remain in the community, SW replied:

> I think it is important, because she lives in a village where there's a fairly high proportion of elderly people in the village who get good support from the 'Good Neighbour Scheme', and as I said earlier they have a caring GP who visits his elderly patients frequently, and no pressure is put on these people to give up their homes. I felt that Mrs M had gone beyond the point where she could be cared for by the village, and by the social services within the community – it was residential care or nothing . . . I felt that she had reached the end of the community caring that was available.

GP/domiciliary services. SW described Mrs M's GP as excellent, and he is one of those paternal type GP's, and he visited her six weekly':

> We would have a monthly meeting at the surgery between the GPs, the Health Visitor and myself, the social worker, and she [Mrs M] would have been discussed at every surgery meeting, usually on the lines of 'what are we going to do about Mrs M?', and he [the GP]

saying that there's no way she can go on looking after herself, and me saying well, we haven't yet got grounds to force her to do anything.

On several occasions SW and the GP discussed the possibility of getting a psychiatrist to do a domiciliary assessment, but:

each time we came to the conclusion that there was no point in getting a psychiatrist to do a domiciliary visit. And even on the day when the community physician came out, he felt the same . . . he felt there was no psychiatrist who would section this lady . . . I know that it is extremely difficult to convince a psychiatrist doing a domiciliary visit with a client like this, who is as articulate as Mrs M, that she is senile to the point that she needs to be admitted to a home because she is a danger to herself and others.

The home help organizer also expressed concern over Mrs M, particularly from the Easter period when the home help hours were increased while Maureen was on holiday, and from July after the home help had first smelt gas in the house:

The home help organizer felt she could not put in more hours for Mrs M, and there was certainly pressure from that direction for me to try to get Mrs M into a home, because she had a lot of help for a long time, and was still deteriorating, and that aspect came into it as well [the justification of persuading Mrs M to accept residential accommodation].

The home help organizer's opinion was that relative to the resources at her disposal, she felt that she could not provide adequate care for Mrs M. There was also the problem of Mrs M's sometimes belligerent and uncooperative behaviour towards the home help to be taken into account.

SW's perspective. I think that it can be seen from the description and illustrations above of SW's relationship with Mrs M's family, her GP, the domiciliary service involved, and her consideration of the community of which Mrs M was a member, that there was considerable pressure on her to 'do something about' Mrs M. I will discuss this in more detail in the next section. First, I think it is important to mention another form of pressure that SW felt herself to be under, which is illustrated by the following:

On the one hand I will support somebody's right to independence to the hilt, but I often picture the headline – '94 YEAR OLD LADY LIVING ALONE, FALLS INTO FIRE, WHAT DID

SOCIAL WORKERS DO ABOUT IT?' . . . I was aware that she would make a classic case of this sort of treatment in the newspapers. I would often have the 1948 Act open before me to see if she might meet the criteria . . . so I found it a very, very difficult case to work with.

The first part of this quotation, 'On the one hand I will support somebody's right to independence to the hilt, but . . . ' I think very accurately summarizes the nature of the difficult role and task that SW had in this case. In the place of her fear of doing nothing and the 'worst' happening and it being scandalized by the press, one could easily change the quotation to:

> I will support somebody's right to independence to the hilt but . . . one must consider the cost (emotional and physical) to her family . . .

or

> but . . . one must consider the high concentration of domiciliary services (but still inadequate) that she was receiving . . .

or

> but . . . her family, her GP, the home help organizer, her neighbours all thought that her behaviour and demands had exceeded what could be accommodated in the community, and therefore she should be 'persuaded' to go into a home.

Analysis

The client's right to self-determination and Mrs M

The crucial area of interest which I shall examine in this case is Mrs M's right to be self-determining 'reflecting an individual's right to manage his own life and to make decisions concerning it' (Butrym, 1976, p. 52); or as Ruth Wilkes has put it, 'freedom from interference, the freedom to be what I am whether anyone likes it, or approves of it or not' (Wilkes, 1981, p. 56). The immediate implication of this is that Mrs M has the right to live her life according to her own wishes, the respect of which should be the social worker's responsibility.

However, almost throughout the whole case, this right of Mrs M to be self-determining was under threat, and was eventually denied her altogether. Although, technically speaking, Mrs M eventually accepted residential care 'voluntarily' (that is Section 47 of the National Assistance Act 1948 was not invoked), she was not free to choose whether or not she wanted to go into residential care. If she had refused, the Act would have been invoked straight away, and so in effect her 'right' to remain at home was taken away from her despite her expressed wish over the months to remain there. It would therefore appear that other criteria relating to her life were eventually deemed to be more important than her right to 'manage her own life'. That is, the effect of her management of her life on herself, but principally, it seems from the interview with SW, on other people (family, community, 'caring services') was judged (by all concerned), to be beyond what was acceptable or tolerable by society's standards and expectations.

So in the context of this case, the value of client self-determination as a right is not a value that exists solely in the context of the relationship between the social worker and the client. Rather, Mrs M's right to self-determination existed also (and perhaps increasingly so), in the context of her relationship with her family, neighbours, local community, her GP, and the demands she was making on the domiciliary services (although these demands were made more on her behalf to meet her needs as perceived by others, rather than her needs as perceived by herself). There were four main, and interrelated considerations that affected Mrs M's right to self-determination.

First, there was the consideration of, and assessment of Mrs M herself by SW, her GP, home help organizer, and in the end, the gas board. As the case progressed, this assessment of Mrs M moved towards the opinion that Mrs M was not capable of looking after herself 'adequately' at home, and there was also an element of risk to herself and others (though undefined by everyone except the gas board) from a gas explosion or fire. From the GP's point of view there was general concern about her health (severe arthritis and a urinary infection), and from SW's and the domiciliary services' perspective there was concern about her ability to look after herself adequately or safely. This concern developed to the point at which it was discussed between SW and the GP as to whether the conditions necessary for invoking Section 47 of the National Assistance Act 1948 might be present. The Act provided the guidelines and justification for denying Mrs M's right to self-determination, although it was agreed that until the gas board disconnected her gas supply that there were not sufficient grounds to invoke the Act, despite everyone's concern.

Second, SW took into account Mrs M's relationship with her two daughters, and the demands that she was making on her neighbours and local community. With regard to her family, the emotional and physical strain on them was an important consideration, particularly from the point at which they said that they could no longer lend practical support to their mother, which had been a major 'prop' to her remaining at home. With regard to Mrs M's neighbours and local community, SW felt that Mrs M's behaviour, her dependency, and the risk she presented eventually surpassed what she felt the local community could or should support.

Third, SW had to consider the adequacy of the support available and given to Mrs M in the community through the social services' department in the light of her deteriorating health and increasing need for services (need that was defined more by the social services than by Mrs M herself). Mrs M's willingness or not to accept available support was also a consideration. Account had to be taken of the home help organizer's view that Mrs M required more home help hours than it was possible to give her. From this, one could argue that a client's right to self-determination in cases similar to Mrs M is also affected by or dependent on an assessment of the domiciliary support required by the client and whether limited resources are sufficient to meet the degree of support required.

Fourth, SW had to consider the wishes and demands of other individuals or agencies concerned. Importantly, both the GP and the home help organizer expressed the opinion that Mrs M was no longer capable of continuing to live in the community. Pressure also came from Mrs M's family for her to go into a 'home', which whilst not having the same 'weight' as the GP's opinion that Mrs M was not really fit to remain at home, or the home help organizer's declaration that it was not possible to give Mrs M the extra home help hours that she needed, was important, if only because of the amount of practical support that they gave to their mother, and which was eventually withdrawn.

As the case progressed, Mrs M's right to self-determination was evaluated in the context of all of these considerations, whose importance increased as Mrs M's mental confusion and physical health appeared to deteriorate, and she was judged to be in need of more and more support. It is, however, interesting to note that a psychiatric assessment of Mrs M was never done, although it is not clear from the interview with SW whether this is because it was decided it would have been totally inappropriate, or because there was little likelihood of it providing the necessary grounds for 'removing' Mrs M, against her will, to residential accommodation. What is clear is that Mrs M's right to self-determination decreases as the concern and demands for 'something to be done' about her increase. The client's right to self-determination appears in this case to be principally a right that may be superseded by consideration of the interests and demands of 'society', which themselves may be in conflict with those of the individual client.

The social worker's role

In the light of the denial of Mrs M's right to self-determination, I would now like to examine more specifically the role played by SW. According to much of the social work literature and theory on values, the social worker's relationship with the client derives from the Kantian imperative of respect for persons, in which the individual's right to self-determination is of central importance. However, as we have seen, SW was also receptive to the needs and demands of 'society', to the network of family/community relationships in which Mrs M lived, which were in conflict with the wishes and the ability of Mrs M to live her life as she wished, without interference.

This conflict also exists (and remains unresolved) within the CCETSW paper on values, where it says that ' . . . in helping with a client's problems, the social worker is morally bound not to do so at the expense of the social norms which apply to all' (CCETSW, 1976). But this could, and does in the case of Mrs M, clash with respecting a person as a self-determining individual, which itself involves assisting the client in the 'pursuit of the actions and policies that he or she wishes to implement' (CCETSW, 1976).

This apparent confusion or contradiction in the social worker's responsibilities is very well highlighted by the case of Mrs M, in which SW's role appears to be based as much on her concern and responsibility to society (including Mrs M's family, local community, the 'health' and 'caring' services), as it was on her concern and responsibility for Mrs M and her wishes.

However, it would be a mistake to view the way Mrs M's right to self-determination diminished and the role of SW simply in terms of a compromise of her right and of the social work value of client self-determination. The reason for this is that central to SW's role and her consideration and assessment of Mrs M was her responsibility to and her responsibility as a local authority social worker for society's interest.

This responsibility is expressed and formalized by Section 47 of the National Assistance Act 1948, and Section 1 of the National Assistance (Amendment) Act 1951, which as long as the grounds specified in S47(1) are satisfied is now more commonly used as it gives authority 'in the interests of that person to remove him without delay'.

Section 47(1) of the 1948 Act states that:

(1)   The following provisions of this section shall have effects for the purposes of securing the necessary care and attention of persons who:

a)   are suffering from grave chronic disease or, being aged, infirm or physically incapacitated, are living in insanitary conditions, and

b)   are unable to devote to themselves, and are not receiving from other persons, proper care and attention (quoted in Norman, 1980).

Specifically, the Act represents SW's statutory responsibilities, and in a more general sense, represents SW's responsibility to society. This responsibility and concern was apparent in the case from the time of the first referral and SW's initial assessment of Mrs M, and provided a continual source of reference.

It is interesting to note, however, that in this case, the Act's interpretation by SW appears to have served more to protect Mrs M's right to self-determination, up until the point when her gas supply was finally disconnected, than it readily provided the grounds for sooner denying her that right. SW remarks in the interview that during her regular meetings with the GP and the health visitor, the GP would argue that Mrs M could no longer continue to look after herself, to which SW would reply that they did not have the grounds to force her to do anything. This remained the situation until the family stopped supporting their mother, and the gas supply was disconnected.

Nevertheless, SW's statutory responsibility, and the pressure from 'society' to 'do something about' Mrs M which increased in intensity as Mrs M's faculties and acceptability decreased, provided the focal point to the relationship between SW and Mrs M.

Essentially, SW's role in the case was one of mediation, that is, she had the task and the problem of balancing her responsibility to 'society', the statutory requirements of her employing agency, with the wishes of the client. The value of the client's right to self-determination has to be seen within this context, which clearly sets limits upon it. SW was necessarily, as part of her job, a party to, and a central figure in assessing and defining these limits to Mrs M's right to self-determination.

To begin with, during the case, she was able to allay the 'need' to deny Mrs M's right to self-determination by persuading her to accept domiciliary support. SW's role here can be seen as mediating or negotiating a compromise between Mrs M and 'society'. That is, she was able to meet the right of Mrs M to stay at home and also, on behalf of society, assist Mrs M to live at what it considered to be an acceptable standard.

However, as the case progressed, SW became more responsive to the concern and demands of Mrs M's family and the other 'health' and 'caring' workers involved with Mrs M and the relationship between Mrs M and the local community. Fairly quickly, as Mrs M's perceived (by others) needs, and the strain she put on her family and community increases, she moves closer to the state that reaches the limit of what 'society' can accept or tolerate, and SW's focus of concern moves more to representing 'society' than representing the wishes and rights of Mrs M.

With respect to Mrs M's right to self-determination, it is not simply a case of it being compromised by the social worker; it is more a case that Mrs M's right was limited to begin with, and SW's job was to represent the concern and demands of society as much as it was to represent the interests and rights of Mrs M. In this case, society's values and expectations outweighed the client's right to self-determination and it was a part of SW's role/task to represent and be instrumental in implementing those values and expectations.

7 Case C: Tracy – Description and Analysis

Description

A housing problem

This case was referred to SW by a social worker from a different part of the case area, when Tracy, mother of three young children, and her husband were evicted from their council house for substantial rent arrears of about £1,000, which included arrears from a previous council tenancy. The district council had been to court and through the Homeless Persons Act 1977, had been discharged of all their obligations to the family: 'So we had a housing problem.'

Following their eviction, Tracy's husband went to live with his father and Tracy and the children moved in with her parents and Tracy's two younger sisters, in their three-bedroomed council house. SW's view of the situation was as follows:

I can see in this case that the Housing Department had made every effort to ensure that the situation should not exist. They had made every best effort to collect rent and had given the couple many opportunities to start paying rent. They had given them several warnings that if they didn't start paying their rent then there would be court proceedings, and so they had in the end taken recourse to law to get it cleared up. I would like to think that perhaps sometimes Housing Departments ought to be flexible enough to say there are situations where they have to say that the need for housing has to override everything else, but I also understand, seeing it in a broader context, that they actually can't do that. I know that even much more tolerant and liberal councils than . . . would have acted in much the same way . . .I have certainly had some success in 'moving' the Housing Department on occasions when I have felt that they have not done everything that they could . . . I know the chap quite well who deals with rent arrears, and have worked with him, and I found him a very warm, humane and caring person who will make every effort to avoid eviction, it's not just a bureaucratic procedure. I know I'm defending them, but I've had some very good experiences where we have avoided eviction and I can see on this occasion why they did what they did, although I don't like it.

Shortly after Tracy had moved to her parents' house she found that she was pregnant again, which added to the fact that her father who had become 'quite ill and depressed', and the obvious tensions that are bound to arise with so many people living in too small accommodation, created considerable pressure in the household:

> Periodically, I would get her mother, very irate and upset on the phone, saying 'you've got to do something', and I would explain that I was doing everything that I could, but there didn't seem to be an awful lot that I could do. Periodically she would actually sling Tracy and the children out, and they would trundle up to the police station and the police station would ring me, and I'd go back to her mum, and usually we patched it up.

> I was getting no movement with the Housing Department, despite the best sympathies from the Letting Office. They were saying, 'Look, the committee's had this taken to court, I can't move'. I also recognised that we were not going to get any movement unless some effort was made to pay off those existing arrears, even if it was only a tiny bit. What I see is a situation where I couldn't negotiate because I'd nothing to negotiate on apart from the moral wrong of someone with three children having no proper home, and I wasn't getting anywhere with that because of the court decision.

SW saw Tracy and her husband together to suggest that it would perhaps help if they started to pay off at least a small part of their arrears, but Tracy's husband rejected the suggestion:

> he said he would not do so, and became very abusive to me and said that I had to get them re-housed, and basically, no, he wasn't going to do anything to help me get them re-housed. So I was still left with the problem of Tracy with three, knocking on four children and the tense situation at home.

The relationship between Tracy and her husband had been breaking down, and since their eviction, contact between them and between him and the children gradually ceased. They were divorced during the time that Tracy was living with her mother.

The deal

> I contacted a Housing Association in — which specialises with single parents, who immediately presented me with two problems. Yes, in principle they could help, but they had very little accommodation and none suitable at the moment; and secondly, that they will only help if they are on the waiting [council] list for housing at some period in the future. So I knew that I had to get

Tracy accepted on to the housing list before the Housing Association were going to accept her. I then went back to the District Council and said this is the problem I've got now, have we got any lee-way here? And they said that if the Housing Association would re-house her, that if she conducted her tenancy satisfactorily over a period of 12 months, and if she paid her rent arrears off at the rate of £1.10 per week, they would re-house her, and her children (but not her husband) at the end of 12 months.

My immediate feeling was one of relief, that I had unlocked the negotiations, I could see a way forward. I suppose it was a bit like the 'miners' before that. We were going in on either side with no movement, and now we'd got to negotiations with pre-conditions. But I wasn't very happy about the pre-conditions. I could see, again trying to see from their point of view, that the conducting of a satisfactory tenancy is going to demonstrate something to them. I can see that they wanted continuation of paying off arrears, and I felt that they were being realistic at the rate that they expected it to be paid off. I wasn't very happy that they expected her to be separated from her husband, that they said that there would be no accommodation for her husband.

In fact, by this time Tracy's relationship with her husband was such that this part of the 'the deal' did not worry Tracy:

I was trying to negotiate between two suppliers of housing . . . Ultimately I think one's there to represent one's client, and to do the best thing by one's client . . . I am certainly happy to argue, disagree, and take up the case until I'm blue in the face, but there comes a point when I have to accept what the other agencies are saying.

Charity
At the same time that SW was negotiating with the Housing Department and the Housing Association, she was trying to find ways to help Tracy pay off her rent arrears:

I approached a number of charities to get money for the rent arrears, which I did by not telling them that they were for rent arrears, because most charities won't fork out for debts. I don't like using charities, I don't think we should need charities. I use them because they can be a way of getting money for extras in some cases, and paying debts in other cases which social security won't do. I deal an awful lot with women who have been left debts by departed spouses. I did with Tracy, and always do, talk to my clients about the possibility and I tend to do it in a fairly cynical way. I tend to say, 'look there are other options of getting money, we're going to have to grovel a bit, how do you feel about that?' Charities have various forms you have to fill in, where you have to make out a deserving case for your client. I usually do that, and then show my client what I've said, and I always dress it up a bit. In fact, it's always something I've had quite a good giggle about with my clients. You'll end up saying things like, 'Mrs Smith is making every effort to cope under enormous emotional stress since her husband left her', when what Mrs Smith might really feel is, 'I'm so glad to get rid of the silly old bugger', or something like that. I suppose that is my way of coping with something I don't really like, and being open about it. And I say to them, this is a means to an end, I'm prepared to go along with it if you're prepared to go along with it.

Social work strategies

I think you develop a number of different strategies for working with different sorts of people, and you know who it's worth confronting because that will get you what you want, what you need for your client. With a statutory agency like Housing or DHSS or the Electricity Board or the Gas Board, I certainly never do anything other than tell the truth. With certain charities I have been known to distort the truth . . . Charities tend to be 'out there', most of them are down in London, and they're faceless. Ironically perhaps, the larger bureaucracies and organisations have stopped being faceless to me because I've worked in . . . for quite a long time. I know all of the letting staff for . . . , and I know a number of the officers at the DHSS. One's also got to bear in mind one's future credibility. If I blew my credibility with reference to one client, I could have blown it with every client I write about in the future. If I write and say that I think this client has an enormous need for urgent re-housing, and they [the Housing Department] don't, then the next time I write and say, 'I think this person is in need of housing for x, y, z, they're less likely to believe me.

It's a game where you've got to use whatever means you can within the limits, such as maintaining credibility, to get whatever you can for your client, and one uses all kinds of strategies. For things like gaining resources, particularly financial resources which are very limited anyway, you learn how to make out a case for getting a particular thing, and you learn how to approach particular individuals . . . Partly it's knowing how to play the game, something of it is about you, yourself. I think you'll find it's a strategy a lot of us use, and we use our patches where we work as well. Over the years you build up your contacts. If you want help from the police, you ring up and find out when Sgt 'So and So' is on, for example, because you know he'll be the most helpful.

Relationship with Tracy
Up to and throughout SW's negotiations with the Housing Department and the Housing Association, Tracy's relationship with SW was very much one of being dependent on SW. Tracy asked SW for help in getting rehoused but played little part herself in the process of negotiation that followed:

> I was doing it on her behalf . . . for a number of reasons, the main one being that a social worker has got more chance arguing against bureaucratic machinery than an individual like Tracy, who cannot read or write, who is not very articulate, and is certainly not very articulate over the telephone, which is what it's going to be likely to involve, because she'd not have the 'wherewithal' to get over to where the offices of the District Council are, which are cross country from where she lives, on no bus route, and for whom making telephone calls anyway means standing in freezing cold telephone boxes pumping 10 pences in, and who had already had her fight of trying not to be evicted in the first place.

> Everything that was going on was so enormous. You know, four kids and no house is like a really big problem and it's the sort of problem you have that you almost feel like hiding your head in the sand. If I owed somebody £500 I'd be very worried about it. If I owed somebody £50,000 I would stop worrying about it because there's no way I can get my hands on £50,000. It's completely beyond my ability to conceptualise, but £500 I can see within my grasp, but not within my grasp enough – and I think it was like that with Tracy and the house. It was so huge that she couldn't see it ever being real.

SW did try to get Tracy to take responsibility for paying the £1.10 rent arrears. SW arranged to meet Tracy every week, on the day she collected her 'Giro', for Tracy to give her £1.10 which SW would send off in a bulk amount to the Housing Department. She arranged to do it this way for two reasons. First, for Tracy to pay it directly herself would have cost her considerably more than £1.10 per week, taking into account the cost of a postal order and postage. Second, it gave SW a way of making sure that Tracy repaid the arrears. However, at one stage this arrangement broke down:

> . . . part of the problem was trying to get the rent arrears from her, that she couldn't connect this £1.10 with a house, and I could; and I had hoped that it would be quite a positive thing, her getting involved with getting re-housed, that that was her bit of responsibility.

... she stopped giving me the money. She kept on coming to see me, but wouldn't give me the money. I discussed it endlessly with her, why she should pay me the money, and she'd always smile and say, 'Yes, I'll give it to you next week'.

SW eventually decided to tackle Tracy about it in the presence of her mother, whom she knew would react strongly to the knowledge that Tracy, was not making the payments, and would put pressure on Tracy to start making them regularly:

I thought about going to tackle her mother about it, without Tracy being there, but I felt that would be wrong, because I was pretty sure that when her mother found out that she wasn't paying me the money, she'd be angry with Tracy, and if I went and talked to her mother about it without Tracy being there, I was 'storing up' a row for Tracy – I was setting that up. Whereas if I went and tackled them together, I was going to be part of that, and could deflect it. It's a dodgey strategy to use, a desperate strategy . . . in a way I think it's quite devious [she did not tell Tracy that she was going to discuss it in front of her mother, or forewarn her mother], but probably less devious than telling her mother behind her back . . . I felt it was the only way I was going to break it open and keep on getting the money. We did at least get that row over whilst I was there, and Tracy started to bring me the money regularly, and I know her mum makes sure that she does. It was a case of the ends justifying the means – there's a lot of that about this case.

The Housing Association eventually found accommodation for Tracy and her children, and Tracy began to take on more and more responsibility for herself, arranging and getting things done:

In practice, when she got the place in . . . and there were all the things that have to be done when you move house, she was great, and suddenly she was right in it . . . and she came to me and said, 'right, I think we've got to do this, this and this', she took over, became autonomous again . . .

The tenancy with the Housing Association went satisfactorily for Tracy and as far as the Housing Department were concerned, and Tracy is now back living in a council house:

I think Tracy saw me as a means to an end, and still does. She sees me a problem solver, and I have, since things have been much smoother, and she is now back in . . . , in a council house with a proper tenancy, and everything's fine, seen much less of Tracy. She

will only come to me if there is a problem so I don't see her that
much now.

Analysis

The social worker's role
In this case SW's relationship with other organizations and agencies
(Housing Association, Housing Department, charity organizations)
appears to be more crucial than the nature of SW's actual relationship
with Tracy. Central to this is the role palyed by SW in mediating on
Tracy's behalf with the Housing Department.

When the Housing Department evicted Tracy and her family from
their council house, and were discharged by the court of their responsibility to provide them with housing. SW saw her main task as helping
Tracy find other accommodation as soon as possible. Tracy's mother's
house was much too small, and the pressures created as a result of
overcrowding and her father's illness, together with a concern to keep
Tracy and her children together, made this the most important task.*
In order to do this SW had to negotiate with the Housing Department
to get them to recognize Tracy's need for accommodation. As a result
of the court action Tracy no longer had a right to council accommodation and so SW had to try to negotiate with the Housing
Department for the reinstatement of Tracy's right. SW's role was that
of a mediator between the Housing Department and Tracy. Tracy herself was relatively powerless to do any of this herself, and I think that
this is the main feature of the relationship between SW and Tracy at
this stage. Apart from the obvious handicap of not being able to read
or write, or have easy access to a telephone, Tracy was also handicapped by the fact that she did not have sufficient 'authority'
(particularly after the court action) that was recognized by the
Housing Department. Neither was she familiar with the bureaucracy
of the Housing Department, knew who to approach, or knew how
best to go about negotiating with them.

SW, on the other hand, although herself handicapped by the court
action in that it limited the response that the Housing Department
were able to give, did know who to approach, had previously worked
with many of the officials on behalf of other clients, and as a social
worker with a 'professional' interest in Tracy and her children, was
regarded by the Housing Department as having the 'authority' to put
forward Tracy's case. Also, and not trivially in respect of Tracy's

*Previous social work involvement with Tracy and her husband had taken
the form of helping (unsuccessfully) them to budget their income.

circumstances, SW had the means of quick and easy communication with the Housing Department.

However, the actual extent of SW's authority or power was limited as can be seen from the fact that the preconditions to the 'ideal' were determined by the Housing Association and, more significantly, by the Housing Department. Although at this stage, Tracy's relationship with her husband was over, SW had no power to insist to the Housing Department that they should provide accommodation for her husband. Nevertheless, SW's intervention and mediation on Tracy's behalf was necessary and crucial in getting her recognition again from the Housing Department and in getting her accommodation.

It is in the context of SW acting on Tracy's behalf and representing her needs to the other agencies that I would now like to examine what values were relevant to this, and how they worked.

Client self-determination and Tracy

First of all, it is interesting to consider the importance (or not) of the value of the 'client's right to self-determination' within the context of the social worker/client relationship (as it is mostly discussed), because in this case it does not appear to be obviously important, or perhaps even relevant. Initially, when the case was referred, Tracy had no power of self-determination or even a recognized right to it in the most important area of her life in which she needed that right, that is to accommodation for herself and her children. Indeed, SW's mediation on her behalf can be seen in terms of restoring that right to her. It was not until the Housing Association had found accommodation for Tracy that she was able to become at all self-determining, and in a position to make decisions about her life. Before that her ability to be self-determining had been severely restricted by her lack of a recognized right to, and a lack of, accommodation. Self-determination is meaningless to an individual without the right and the ability (both of which in the context of this case are dependent on the recognition of others) to satisfy basic human needs. The need for accommodation is one such need, and if the relevant supplier of accommodation does not recognize that right, then a major area of one's 'right to manage [one's] own life and to make decisions concerning it' (Butrym, 1976, p. 52) is restricted and denied, and hence too is one's right and ability to be self-determining. So in as much as the client's right to self-determination is relevant to this case it is so in the context of Tracy's relationship with the Housing Department rather than her relationship with SW. The latter relationship is, in fact, based on getting recognition from the Housing Department for Tracy's needs, and it is not until that is done that

Tracy has any significant power and opportunity to be self-determining.

It is also interesting that, because of the legal sanctions taken by the Housing Department, this value had to be negotiated. Its value in itself as a right was, under the circumstances of the court action taken by the Housing Department, secondary to the Housing Department's authority to, in effect, restrict Tracy's ability and right to be self-determining.

Ends and means
Part I described what the concept of 'respect for persons' meant, and its importance to social work. Accepting the qualifications and problems relating to 'personhood' and 'rationality', I described respect for persons as a universal right, that is, it does not serve only to identify the rights that appertain to people when they become clients of social workers. It applies to all people, and thereby includes colleagues, individuals, and members of other organizations and agencies, that the social worker might deal with. It is not something that is more relevant in some relationships than others. One should always: 'Act in such a way that you always treat humanity whether in your own person or in the person of any other, never simply as a means, but always at the same time as an end' (Kant, I. in Paton 1949, p. 91).

However, when SW applied to a number of charities for financial aid, but did not tell them that it was intended to help pay Tracy's rent arrears, SW was simply using them as a means to an end.

Similarly, in setting up the situation in which she brought up the matter of Tracy failing to pay the £1.10 per week in rent arrears in front of her mother and without forewarning Tracy or her mother, SW was using them both as a means to end, principally her mother.

In both cases the values that SW adhered to were instrumental to the purpose, and the justification for each action was its result, its utility.

With regard to the 'charities', the purpose was to get money from them to help pay off Tracy's arrears, and the means of deceiving the charities about what the grants would be used for was justified by the result that a couple of charities did award Tracy small grants.

With regard to setting up the discussion in front of her mother of Tracy's failure to keep up with paving the £1.10 per week arrears, the purpose was for Tracy's mother to put pressure on Tracy to keep up with her arrears, but in SW's presence so that she could 'deflect the row' that would ensue between Tracy and her mother. Once again SW's means, of not forewarning Tracy or her mother about her intentions, were justified by the outcome. Tracy's mother did have a 'row' with Tracy but SW did manage to deflect it, and from then on Tracy paid her rent arrears regularly.

Obviously, both these examples were important to achieving the end of Tracy being accepted by the Housing Department and being given a council house. In as much as this was eventually achieved then one can say that the 'end' justified the 'means'.

If one looks at SW's actions in terms of 'positive freedom' (self-determination) then one can see how it is possible to justify SW's actions in the instance of her setting up the confrontation between Tracy and her mother. The denial of respect in that instance was just-ified by the future increase in Tracy's self-determination when she got her own accommodation (and her mother got her home back).

In the case of SW's attitude towards the charities she applied to, this justification cannot be made. Although Tracy benefited, the charities which gave financial help were simply deceived, which raises the question that I mentioned regarding the use of self-determination as positive freedom, and its vulnerability to manipulation and coercion, and also the extent to which it is justifiable; in this case not in terms of manipulating the client, but of manipulating others in the interests of the client.

Interestingly, what also emerges from the case is that there are restraints on the use of this instrumental strategy, and that it cannot be used universally, in all situations, or with all individuals, agencies or organizations. However, the key factor here is the need to maintain 'credibility' in the eyes of the individuals or organizations (rather than moral restraint) with whom SW is in regular or close contact, such as the DHSS, the gas and electricity boards, and, of course, the Housing Department. Significantly, although SW felt that Tracy had a moral right to housing, her approach to the negotiations with the Housing Department seem to have been based as much on her understanding of, and sympathy with, their perspective as it was in representing her client's perspective, although in the end SW felt that her main task (in this case at least) was to represent the needs of her client.

It is also interesting to note that it is not simply the size of, or the nature of, the organization that is the crucial factor in deciding 'strategy', but it is the personal contacts within them that SW has made as a social worker. On this basis, SW used the 'faceless' charities from

London instrumentally, but not organizations with whom she regularly dealt with and depended on and with whom it was important to maintain her integrity, her credibility.

Central to SW's approach to social work, as seen in this case, and of understanding how values work in social work practice is the element of applying the right strategy for dealing with 'different sorts of people', of making the right kind of case for getting a particular thing, within which values (e.g. respect for persons) are secondary (within limits of credibility) to the goal. In other words, the dominant ethic is utilitarian - the moral worth of a particular action rests on its consequences rather than the implicit rightness or wrongness of the action, in which moral worth would be related to the act or behaviour itself, as is exemplified by 'respect for persons'.

8 Conclusions

Members of a profession have obligations to their clients, to their employers, to each other, to colleagues in other disciplines and to society (BASW, 1970).

Whilst the case studies cannot be taken to be in any way conclusive, they do illustrate something of the complexities and the actual meaning of the quotation above. Concentrating on the two cases described in detail, the obligations of the social worker to the client, employers, to their colleagues in other disciplines, and to society, all played crucial parts (but different in both cases) in determining what happened to the social work values involved, and in our understanding of what happened. Four main points emerge from the cases of 'Mrs M' and 'Tracy'.

First, in practice, the way in which social work values work and are used is determined by the social worker's obligations to other people, organizations, and society according to the extent that they are interested in, concerned, or affected by the interests and actions of the client. In both cases, 'respect for persons' and the client's right to self-determination were contingent in their use and applicability to the particular context of the case, in this sense.

For example, in the case of Mrs M, her right to self-determination was determined, and in the end limited by SW's obligations to her statutory responsibilities, and her consideration of and obligations to represent the interests, concerns and needs of Mrs M's GP, family, community, and the adequacy of the available domiciliary services. All of these concerns and obligations were formalized through SW's employing agency's expectations of her.

Second, and closely related to the first point, is that the way in which values 'worked' and were 'used' was dependent on the specific nature of the role or task of the social worker involved, whether statutorily, agency, or professionally defined. For example, in the case of Tracy, the task of getting Tracy recognized by the Housing Department as having a legitimate right to housing determined SW's use of the value of respect for persons in dealing with other agencies. In this case the end justified the means.

Third, in both cases the social worker's role was that of a mediator or negotiator between the client and others ('society'), although the exact nature, expectations and outcome of this role were different in both cases. The values of respect for persons and client self-determination operated within this context. They did not exist either in consideration or effect, independent of or 'above' this context in the sense of giving a positive ethical instruction as to what the social work role or task and relationship with the client should be.

This social work role in both cases is illustrated in Figure 8.1.

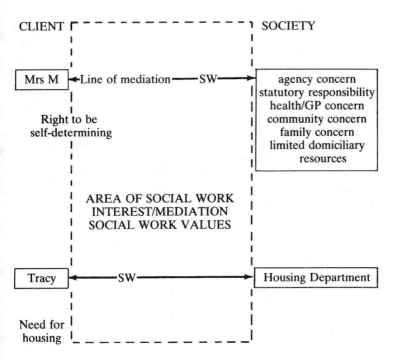

Figure 8.1 The social work role

In the case of Mrs M, the diagram shows the considerable extent of society's interest in her, in terms of concern for her welfare and health, prompted by the effects of her behaviour, and the risks and demands that she presented to others (family, community, social services) which eventually outweighed her wish and 'right' to live her life as she wished. SW's initial task was to support Mrs M in the community, if possible (according to society's standards and expectations), which in effect meant that Mrs M's right to be self-determining was questioned and limited right at the outset. As her 'condition' was perceived to grow worse, concern was heightened to the extent that her 'right' to independence was eventually taken away.

At this point, SW was basically representing society's concern to Mrs M, although initially at least, she had recognized and represented Mrs. M's right to be self-determining, to society, to her family, and to her GP, who had questioned Mrs. M's right to be self-determining quite early on. Eventually, though (indicated in the diagram by the position of SW being closest to 'society'), she came more to represent the concern and wishes of society as its concern and demands increased in response to Mrs M's perceived 'risk' to herself and others, and the increasing demands (as perceived by the carers) she was placing on the 'caring' services.

In the case of Tracy, the situation is simpler (and not so 'loaded' against the client) in that SW is mediating only between the Housing Department and the client. The area and extent of society's concern was not anything like as great as in the case of Mrs M in that Tracy was not making demands on anyone and was not the object of any direct concern apart from her mother and SW. SW's role was to keep the family together, which meant helping Tracy to find accommodation for herself and her children, by getting the Housing Department to acknowledge Tracy's plight. In this case the social worker's role was one of fostering the client's right and ability to be self-determining rather than denying it, as was the eventual situation in the case of Mrs M.

One crucial difference between the two cases, which affects how the values 'worked' in both, and what the social worker's role was in both, lies in the source and nature of the original referrals. Mrs M did not refer herself; she was referred by her daughter as a problem, an object of concern to be acted upon. One could consider her family and her local community as becoming more the clients as the case progresses, whilst Mrs M becomes more just the focus of attention. This perspective clearly shows the rights of the community as being in conflict with the rights of the individual.

Tracy, although referred by another social worker, did ask for help herself (which Mrs M never did), and in this case the problem to be acted upon was the Housing Department's legally sanctioned denial of housing for Tracy. That is, the focus of SW's attention was the 'problem' rather than Tracy herself, and the social worker was engaged in fostering Tracy's ability and opportunity to be self-determining.

Fourth, both cases illustrate in different ways how values are used instrumentally, in which the dominant ethic is utilitarian rather than deontological. This is obvious in the case of Tracy in which the moral worth of an action rested on its consequences rather than its inherent moral worth. It was also the case regarding Mrs M, in which her right to self-determination (as negative freedom, based on the Kantian 'respect for persons') was limited by a utilitarian ethic in which a consideration of and for the greater 'good' of the community/society, justified the denial of the individual's right to be self-determining.

In the case of Mrs M one could argue that SW was acting on behalf of the state by implementing paternalistic legislation which required her to constrain Mrs M's freedom in what was purportedly her own, as well as society's best interests. This owes more to the concept of positive freedom and is thus based on a utilitarian rather than a deontological ethic.

What clearly emerges from this study is that in order to begin to understand values in practice one has to examine the nature of the social work role and task. It is inadequate simply to conclude that 'professional values' may sometimes be compromised or superseded by other considerations, because this ignores the important relationship between society and the social worker, which the study suggests is of central importance in defining and understanding the relationship between the social worker and the client.

Therefore in order to understand social work values in practice it is necessary to examine the nature of this relationship between society and the social worker, which is the purpose of Part III.

PART III
VALUES IN CONTEXT

As indicated in Part II, Part III consists of an examination of the nature of the relationship between society and the social worker. Social work values are examined in the light of this analysis, in order to attempt to understand their role, importance, what they mean, and how they 'work', in the context of local authority-based social work practice.

9 Social Work and Society

The state isn't some abstract thing, the state is the social worker knocking on someone's door . . . (Bill Jordan, *Social Work Today*, 3.9.84, p. 13).

The 'social' in social work

In the *Concise Oxford Dictionary* and the Collins *New English Dictionary*, the word 'social' is defined as 'concerned with the mutual relations of human beings', and 'affecting public interest'. If one applies these definitions to 'social' work, then one has an activity which affects, or is in the public interest. However, as it is, this is an unsatisfactory definition of social work in that it could include many activities which would not normally be considered to be social work, such as 'middle classes running jumble sales . . . scoutmasters taking difficult boys up mountains', and in a more professional sense, it could be used to describe the work of 'health visitors or GP's talking about money problems' (Anderson, 1982, p. 9). These activities are all 'social', and although they refer to the general area in which social workers work, as well as the medium through which they work, they do not specify or clarify what 'social' means in the context of local authority-based social work.

If one turns to BASW for clarification, they offer the following definition:

> The purposeful and ethical application of personal skills in inter-personal relationships directed towards enhancing the personal and social functioning of an individual, family, group or neighbour-hood, which necessarily involves using evidence obtained from practice to help create a social environment conducive to the well-being of all (BASW, 1977, p. 19).

Whilst this 'pocket' definition may read well, on reflection, it could apply to many kinds of 'social' activities, not the least as Anderson (1982, p. 10) points out, 'a high class brothel keeper could accept that model if she could make sense of it.'

Rather than starting with a description of the activity itself, in order to find out what social work is, it is first necessary to relate it to, and put it in the context of the society in which we live and from which it derives its existence.

Two features common to all societies are that there are 'norms which are basic to all societies which enable people to relate to each other' (Fowler, 1975, p. 90); and the recognition of some varying (between different cultures) degree of responsibility for those of its members in need. Our society is no exception to this, and has organized various services provided by the community which express this sense of obligation to its members that it defines and accepts as being in need. Titmuss (1958, p. 39) describes this process as 'manifestations first of society's will to survive as an organic whole . . . '

Around areas of communal interest, for example, the maintenance of social order, child-rearing practices, and care of the elderly and handicapped, social institutions establish themselves. Some of these directly assume 'communal responsibility' and operate on behalf of society through the establishment of state agencies. Local authority social services departments are an example of one such agency, whose task it is to take an interest in certain kinds of behaviour and the social conditions of recognized individuals within society.

Within this, the social work task and its objectives reflect societal norms, for example, certain standards about bringing up children. Social work, then, is basically normative and social workers, and for example teachers and psychiatrists, are 'socialising agents' (Fowler, 1975, p. 91)

Anderson (1982) indentifies the social work task as dealing with people who are in conflict with some norms in society, as a feature which separates the 'social' in social work from more general forms of 'social' work. He argues that 'the essence of the social work task is the resolution of that conflict' (1982, p. 10). If there is not a conflict of norms, then social work is not being done, although one may be working socially.

Howe (1979, p. 32) also argues that the 'social' in social work should be understood by taking it to refer to the socially sanctioned nature of social work. That is, society sanctions certain members or agents (social workers) to take an interest in the conditions and behaviour of some of its members (clients). This interest or intervention may be at the request of the client who acknowledged the interest and expertise of the social worker as appropriate to the resolution of his/her problem; it may be because of a request from others, as in the case of probation.

In a similar vein, Fowler (1975, p. 89) describes social work as:

best seen as a continuum having, at the one end, help mobilised out of a sense of caring and recognition of responsibility to the individual in need, and at the other end, help which is mobilised because of the perceived threat to the established order, characterised by the criminal, mentally ill, unemployed etc.

Such is the case where the individual (client) is defined as rejecting or being in conflict with some generally accepted norm of behaviour. Two important points emerge from this description of social work: 'who defines the client?' and the 'role and importance of the part played by agency function'.

Who defines the client?

'Who' becomes a client is largely a socially determined matter, that is, the individual's behaviour, either because he/she has a 'social' problem, or is a problem to others, is of social interest:

> Never simply is it a matter between a social worker and the client . . . what social workers do, and who they do it with are socially determined matters. Social work might therefore be seen as an activity carried out under social auspices (Howe, 1979, p. 33).

Timms and Timms (1977, p. 17) argue in a similar vein, 'the "social" in their title [referring to social workers] refers to the auspices under which they work, rather than to their field (working as it were with things social).' Fowler (1975, p. 91) makes the point more forcibly when he says, 'Social work ceases to be such when it fails to reflect the norms of the society it serves.' And similarly, Nokes (1967, p. 111) writes:

> not withstanding the welfare practitioners' desire for professional autonomy, the welfare professions are rooted in the values of wider society . . . there can be no complete withdrawal from the essential social nature of welfare practice.

The following example illustrates the main force of the argument presented above.

When someone has a toothache, the ache exists solely within the person, and its origins lie solely within the person (the decayed tooth). It is not (at least not directly) the result of, or dependent on, other people. It is matter of conern only for the sufferer and the dentist. Similarly, the dentist's knowledge base and task of alleviating the toothache are not socially based, or carried out under 'social auspices'. However, in comparison a social worker's response to a delinquent teenager is totally dependent on other people. First, it requires a 'socially determined' definition of who and what is or is not delinquent; and second, the social worker's involvement with the delinquent is based on a social and moral response to the delinquency. That is, the creation of the 'social worker', the 'delinquent', and the social worker's response and responsibility to the delinquent all depend on and are derived from other people.

Without this 'social interest', argues Howe, 'the individual's behaviour and conditions can be of no concern to the social worker qua social worker' (1979, p. 32).

However, none of the argument above in any way assumes (or is dependent on) that who or what is defined as a social problem is necessarily commonly agreed or recognized. In the first place, certain specific groups within society (e.g. the government of the day) may be responsible for, and have the power and influence to define social problems.

Second, who or what is defined as a social problem may change over time and in differing circumstances. What is important here is that 'human conduct and social reactions to it are political and moral in character' (Howe, 1979, p. 33).

The importance of agency function
The second major consideration which comes out of this description of social work is the concept of agency function. Largely through the writings of the Functionalist School of Social Work, the concept of agency function has attempted to describe the nature of the relationship between the individual (client), social worker, and society. As the argument above has indicated, social workers are by definition neither autonomous nor private practitioners, just as clients are not 'abstracted individuals simply choosing between commodities' (Timms, 1983, p. 81). Jessie Taft, one of the people who originally developed the concept of agency function, wrote of the agency as 'a background which holds both worker and client in a larger reality' (Taft, 1944 in Timms, 1983, p. 81). In this 'larger reality', the social worker is identified primarily with the tasks which society has sanctioned the agency to carry out, rather than with the client: 'the caseworker's responsibility on the other hand, real as it is, must first of all be to the agency and its functions; only as agency does he meet this client professionally' (Taft in Smalley, 1959, p. 109).

So, the 'social' in social work refers not just to its concern with social relationships, the relationship between the individual and society, but to the sanction and auspices for its practice. Social work has a social base and is not just a matter between social worker and client.

Winnicott (1964, p. 109) describes the relationship between social work and agency function in terms of agency function having the role of a parent figure. For example, in child care she defines the agency's function as parental, expressing the sense of responsibility that exists in the community towards children. Similarly, she argues that the primary social function of probation workers is to offer their clients a corrective experience of authority which is 'reasonable, consistent and based on concern for the other person' (Winnicott, 1964, p. 109).

Timms has also written about the central importance of agency function in social work:

> The agencies are established to carry out such broad social functions as healing and rehabilitation in the case of hospitals, ensuring good parental care in the case of children's departments of the local authority . . . the most important aspect of agency function is that it constitutes the meeting point of social worker and client, it is what brings them together and gives meaning and sustenance to their continued contact (Timms, 1954, pp. 8-9).

Howe puts even greater emphasis on the importance of agency function by suggesting that social work has no identity outside agency function, denying it any degree of autonomy to determine its own identity, its task, who is the client, and the relationship with the client:

> To have social work embedded in society may be to preclude it having any discrete existence outside its relationship with various social agencies. The work of social work emerges out of social processes, the outcome of which determines who the clients are to be and how they are to be handled . . . Inbred with the 'social' at all levels, social work is unable to disentangle itself from the social world without ceasing to be social work (Howe, 1979, p. 35).

Social work's lack of power to 'determine' itself is echoed by Johnson (1977) who describes two basic areas of social work which are outside the control of social workers. First, there is the determination of clients and their needs (the problem); and second, the character of the responses available (the method). Both of these are identified and determined by the state.

Finally, Warham (1977, p. 52) writes that 'real' social work (referring to local authority social service departments) can only be defined in relation to the social context in which social workers find themselves: 'It is not of a kind which is at the discretion of the profession itself to determine without reference to the essentially public nature of the situations in which social workers are employed.'

The argument here is that social work values operate within the 'agency' and its socially defined and sanctioned concerns. As such analysis of values in social work must relate to the context in which they function, and must seek to locate their role and importance within this context. In order to do this it is necessary to examine in detail the nature of the social worker's role within this 'agency' 'socially sanctioned' context.

10 The Social Work Role

Social work knowledge and values – creating the subject
Whilst social work draws on a number of different disciplines within the social sciences, which attempt to create an 'objective' picture of the individual and society (for example as in psychology and sociology), social work is essentially concerned with producing a knowledge of the individual as a 'subject': 'Social work produces a subject in objective knowledge' (Philp, 1979, p. 91). Although, in creating the subject, social work draws on other disciplines, it differs from them and is not reducible to them because of its purpose of creating the 'subject'. The 'subject' itself is characterized by universal rather than individual subjectivity, and this applies to all individuals but no one individual in particular.

Social work values are central to the creation of the subject, providing the 'subjective' focus within which the social worker operates. Here the most basic value or 'prerequisite to having values at all' (Plant, 1970) is respect for persons (individualization), the 'recognition of the value and dignity of every human being irrespective of status, sex, age, belief, or contribution to society' (BASW, 1975). This value base requires the social worker to appreciate how the individual perceives and experiences his/her world. The 'subject' and the social worker's relationship with the subject are based on 'the inherent worth of man . . . independent of his actual achievements or behaviour' (Butrym, 1976, p. 43); 'respect is owed to a man irrespective of what he does, because he is a man' (Plant, 1970, p. 12).

The social worker, on the one hand faced with, for example, an 'objectified' vandal, and on the other with a legal discourse, attempts to present the underlying subjectivity of the vandal. The social worker describes the underlying character, the essential good:

> the authentic and the unalienated . . . In doing so he is producing a picture of the vandal as a subject who is not immediately visible, but who exists as a potential, a possibility, a future social being (Philp, 1979, p. 99).

Interestingly, Biestek (1961) argues along similar lines, though from a theological standpoint in the last few pages of his book, particularly where he describes the value of 'individualization': 'the recognition of and understanding of each client's right and need to be treated as an individual who has unique qualities . . . ' (1961, p. 136).

In the conclusions to their research into practice theories of social work, Curnock and Hardiker (1979) describe the nature of the social work task in relation to assessing referrals, and writing social enquiry reports:

> however typical or general a client's situation and problems seem to be, a way has to be found of finding out what they mean to that particular person. Individualisation is the theoretical key which helps us to be rather more specific about the 'making sense process' (Curnock and Hardiker, 1979, p. 165).

Here, they are referring to the importance of creating the 'subject', of understanding the subjective experience of the individual, central to which is the value of individualization (deriving from respect for persons). They go on to describe how, in order to make an assessment or come to any conclusions about the individual, it is necessary to individualize the presenting problem (crime, non-accidental injury, mental illness etc.) in relation to the client's life situation, such as 'strengths and stresses in his personal or social circumstances' (1979, p. 165).

Whilst acknowledging the radical critique of individualization (respect for persons) (e.g. Statham, 1978, pp. 25-8) Curnock and Hardiker describe the concept as helping social workers to make sense of some of the processes that they are involved in as they make assessments as part of their social inquiries.

Pearson (1975, p. 128) suggests that 'social work emphatically embraces human subjectivity and regards itself as a carrier of the human tradition of compassion.' In terms of the relationship which the social worker has with the individual and with the state, social work can be seen as 'straddling a split' (Philp, 1979, p. 92) between subjective states of the individual and their objective statuses. Subjective states may be characterized, for example, by pain, suffering, need, love, hate; and objective statuses may be characterized by, for example, old age, handicap, mental illness, debts or crime. The objective status of an individual is the result of social processes within society that identify areas of behaviour as being of social interest, to which agency function responds. Against this (although still within the context of 'agency'), social work knowledge and its ensuing principles require the social worker to consider and represent (though not necessarily to act as advocate for the subjective state of the socially identified and defined individual. The knowledge/value base of the social worker transforms individual subjective states and objective statuses to create a 'social subject' (Philp, 1979, p. 92). Importantly, from the point of view of a study of values in social work, the subject is characterized by his/her capacity to be a self-determining, responisble and sociable citizen (Plant, 1970, ch. 3).

Limitations

Both Philp and Howe have pointed out that the individual can only be regarded as a subject if 'he does not have any overpowering objective or narcissistic characteristics' (Philp, 1979, p. 92); and 'if that [socially identified] behaviour becomes too far removed from the way things ought to be, it is dealt with as alien, threatening and in need of sharp control' (Howe, 1979, pp. 42-3).

So, the social worker's relationship with the individual (client) is limited, that is, society's commitment to allowing a subjective picture of the individual to emerge from within their objective status is tolerated only within socially sanctioned boundaries. The social worker cannot speak for those whose objective status overwhelms their subjectivity.

The objective description and status of a child abuser or 'experienced' delinquent may well outweigh the social worker's 'subjective' interest in the person, their 'inherent worth', their 'value and dignity', irrespective of their achievements or behaviour, and their right to be self-determining. The subjective description will not be heard when:

> the objective characteristics of the feared outweigh all the subjective possibilities . . . social work is allocated those whose objective status is not too threatening . . . it cannot operate, it cannot make people when an individual's act has removed him from the right to be perceived as human (Philp, 1979, p. 98).

For example, the social worker cannot defend the mass murderer or the 'florid psychotic', because their objective status is so great as to overwhelm their subjectivity. In the case of an adolescent in court for his fourth 'breaking and entering' offence, and who has already been in care, his objective status will probably be considered greater than his subjective characteristics or potential by the magistrates, and he will probably be sent to a detention centre or borstal.

However, the socially sanctioned boundaries within which social work takes place are not static, and there is a constant tension etween social work, dealing with people who are objectively defined s being of interest and concern to society; and dealing with those ame people in 'the subjective' as individuals worthy of individual respect' and 'concern'. This tension becomes apparent in what seem o be society's contradictory expectations of social work, such as care nd control, although as Fowler (1975) and Davies (1981) point out, oth are integral and important social work functions in the context f agency function.

Mediating between subjective and objective

Essentially, social work performs a mediating role in society, engaged hrough its knowledge of the subject of which its values are the focal oint, in the recognition of social potential. As Pearson (1975a . 135) argues 'social work theory and practice strive to give the leviant a voice', although this task, as we have seen, may be limited:

> It [social work] negotiates on behalf of the mad, bad, and the
> stigmatised; between those who have been excluded from power
> and those who have the power to exclude . . . between the sound
> in body . . . and the handicapped, between the law abiding and the
> law breaking . . . and the sane and the borderline (Philp, 1979,
> p. 97).

Philp (1979) describes social work as developing historically between wo discourses, the dicourse of wealth and the discourse of poverty. The first 'form' of social work was composed of a discourse of charity n which the charity worker mediated between the privileged and the oor, representing the humanity of the privileged to the poor, and the essential 'goodness' of the poor to the privileged. At present social work 'occupies the space between the respectable and the deviant' Philp, 1979, p. 96). In the same vein, Howe describes social work as operating on the edges of different worlds, the world of the individual nd the world of those with the power to legislate how behaviour is to e judged: 'The social worker mediates and translates between these arious worlds' (Howe, 1979, p. 43).

Davies (1981, p. 141) has illustrated the mediation role of the social worker as in Figure 10.1. He describes the role of the social worker as one of reconciliation in which the social worker is concerned with maintaining the individual and society, and with negotiating the nterdependent relationship between the individual and society. According to Davies, the 'maintenance strategy' has two main aspects. On the one hand, social workers are employed by the state to control nd monitor excesses of behaviour which society classes as deviant. For example, social workers are involved in preventing non-accidental njury, the compulsory admission to hospital of mentally ill

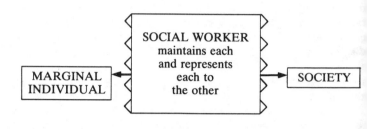

Figure 10.1   The mediation role of the social worker

individuals, and recommending the reception of delinquent childre
into care. Another aspect to mediation is a concern with 'amelioratir
the living conditions of those who are finding it difficult to cop
without help' (Davies, 1981, p. 38). So, for example, the soci
worker might work to improve the quality of life for unemploye
teenagers, handicapped people, and individuals with emotional an
relationship difficulties: 'All of these acts are intended to contribu
to a smooth-running society, to maintain it' (Davies, 1981, p. 138

The creation of subjects is essential to both of these aspects o
mediation, and also to a further aspect of mediation described b
Philp (1979). In presenting the potential of the subject, the soci
worker is suggesting that the objective status, which has cast tl
individual as a client in the first place, can be integrated into tl
subject. This integration is necessary, he argues, for the return to tl
individual of their full discursive rights. The objective status remove
from the client the rights to normal discourse and can only b
returned by a process (of negotiation or mediation) whereb
subjective status is gradually returned. This role of the social work
and the process of mediation can be well illustrated in symbolic for
(adapted from Philp, 1979).

If a child *A* commits an offence *B* and is brought before the cour
he will be seen (legally) through his objective status as *B(a)*. That i
he will be seen principally as an offender and only second as a
individual. If the offence is not serious, the social worker may be ab

to present a picture of the subject (in the court report) that transforms $B(a)$ into $A(b)$, so that the offence is seen as secondary to the individual's subjective characteristics. If the offence is more serious, or previous offences have been committed, the child may be made the subject of supervision, in which the child's B status will fade, and he will again be accepted as A if after a time he does not commit offence B again during this period. The social worker may use various forms of 'treatment' which help the social worker to present a 'scientific or objective picture of the process of change in a client to other discourses – essentially those "explanations" serve to change the client's status from $B(a)$ to $A(b)$' (Philp, p. 101).

The length of the whole process of integration and the extent to which it can be completed, given the limitations to the acceptance of the 'subjective', depends on the nature and extent of the objective status. This can be illustrated by the following examples.

If someone asks a social worker to liaise with one of the fuel boards over the non-payment of a bill (and perhaps a threat of disconnection), probably to try to negotiate some arrangement of weekly repayments, then the whole process would most likely be fairly short and straight-forward.

If, however, a parent is suspected of maltreating their child, then the anxiety, fear and censure present in such a referral is such that the social worker's involvement is liable to be quite a lengthy process.

In the process of integration the social worker, as well as trying to negotiate the client's objective characteristics into a subject, may also be trying to integrate them into wider society. The social worker attemps to change perceptions both in the client and in those around the client:

> The more powerful those characteristics are, the more likely it is that the process will take place with the individual, the less strong the more easily will the integration be effective in those around the client (Philp, p. 101).

Summary

The role of the social worker is to speak for the 'subject' within the 'object'. He/she is sanctioned by society, through his/her employing agency to speak for the subject, and for someone who can return again to their subjective status although, for example, in the case of the elderly and the handicapped this may not reduce or nullify their objective characteristics.

The extent to which this task is possible though, is limited by society, its norms, and its expectations of social services agency; it is also a part of the social worker's role to represent those norms and expectations. So although it is the social worker's role to represent the 'subjective' characteristics of the individual, it is not necessarily her role to act as an advocate for and on behalf of the client. It is the social worker's role to represent and translate the subjective experience of the individual to society, and society's norms and expectations to the individual, and maintain a 'society'-determined balance between the two. Hence the social worker's role essentially includes aspects of both care and control.

Who, in the first place, becomes a client is largely determined by society, and depending on the extent of the individual's objective status, the social worker may be acting for society more than the individual.

Social work values (principally 'respect for persons') are of central importance to this description of social work, because they are of central importance to the creation of the subject. Without values there can be no subject; without the subject, there can be no social work. However, this is not to say that social work's values are necessarily always the dominant values in evidence. Society's values may, in fact, overrule them, and do at least determine the extent to which their 'voice' can be heard in the creation of the subject. Society also determines the extent to which the social worker is able, or is sanctioned to promote the expressed wishes of the client.

For example, although social work places a high value on promoting (in theory) the client's right to self-determination, as has been argued and illustrated above, no such right is tenable in an absolute form. It is limited by the interests of 'parties' other than the client, in which the social worker's role may be one of social control through regulating the acceptable or permissible extent of client self-determination. The client's right to self-determination is also limited by the social worker's concern for the interests of the client even where this may contradict the client's own wishes (self-determination as positive freedom justifying the denial of self-determination as negative freedom).

Although the commitment to self-determination is an important one in social work value theory, in practice, social workers have to recognize and work within a social context in which some of their tasks are designed to monitor and procure social control. Clarke with Asquith comment that: 'Social workers perhaps sense that in a way they are expected to be on both sides of the self-determination social control, and self-determination – paternalism boundaries at the same time' (1985, p. 40).

As has been argued, social work is not an autonomous or independent profession: it exists under social auspices and as such its clients and its role with them is sanctioned and determined by society through agency function. This is the context in which social work values exist and operate.

11 'Values are not Instrumental to some Purpose, but are Expressive of some Ultimate Conviction'?

The main argument has been that in order to examine and understand social work values, it is necessary to understand the nature of social work and the social worker's relationship with society. It is not sufficient simply to look at values in the context of the relationship between the social worker and the client. That is, it is not sufficient to consider only the theoretical or 'professional' description of social work values as if they existed in a 'casework vacuum'.

Part II and III, by practice illustrations and theoretical argument showed that 'outside factors', the context in which the interaction between social worker and client takes place, plays an important role in determining and understanding the place and practical operation of social work values.

In Part III, the main function of social work has been described as creating 'subjects', central to which lies the basic social work value of 'respect for persons' (individualization).

However, in this description the way in which values are used and work is essentially 'instrumental'. That is, they are instrumental to achieving the end of creating the subject. It is this task of the social worker and social work values which describes and determines (within agency-defined limits) the nature of the social worker's relationship with the client.

The 'end' of creating the subject is itself sanctioned and determined by agency function which reflects the norms and expectations of society. Within this, respect for persons provides the 'means' by which the social worker creates and presents a picture of the 'subjective' characteristics of the client as an individual.

As has been described in Part III, there are limits to the extent to which this can be achieved, but within this description of social work values are basically instrumental to the purpose, and appear to be no more than a 'means to an end'. They are not 'absolute' imperatives, as was illustrated in the case of Mrs M's limited rights to self determination.

However, this particular description raises the important question: 'Is this all that there is to say about social work values?' Or are values, as Ruth Wilkes claims, 'not instrumental to some purpose, but expressive of some ultimate conviction'? (Wilkes, 1981, p. 64).

The answer, not surprisingly perhaps, is more complex than can be formulated by an either – or question. The question, though, is important because behind this claim of Wilkes lie many generally held basic assumptions about social work as a 'profession' with a clear set of values, and it is this description of social work that is challenged in Part III.

Deontological and utilitarian values

The conclusions to Part I briefly described how local authority-based social work is founded on a utilitarian concept of need. Clarke with Asquith (1985, p. 70) argue that certainly since the Seebohm Report (1968) social work has been based on such a conception. The report called for a reorganization of the personal social services to attract more resources, and to meet needs on the basis of the overall requirements of the family, or individual. Having a 'need' implies lacking a 'good' whose possession is, in an important way, conducive to 'happiness'. From this it is the task of social work to attempt to maximize the well-being of individuals and that of the community as a whole. Similarly Martin Davies (1981, pp. 137–8), in describing the role of social work as 'maintenance': ['Social workers'] . . . acts are intended to contribute to a smooth running society', also appears to be describing a strong utilitarian commitment to the development of social work.

Again, Ruth Wilkes has written:

consciously or unconsciously, social work thinking is for the most part, sympathetic with utilitarian modes of thought in that the worth of a policy or action is measured against its tendency to produce 'good' results (Wilkes, 1981, p. 63).

A description of social work principally depicting the role of 'respect for persons' as being instrumental in the creation of subjects would appear to fit neatly into a description of social work with a strong utilitarian base, in which the 'end' rather than any moral obligation is the justification for the act. And it certainly accords with a description of social work as an activity which is practised under the auspices and sanctions of society.

However, this view of social work and its values contrasts sharply with the more 'traditional' description and the role of social work values, particularly respect for persons, as described in Part I. An assertion of the value of each individual person clearly contrasts with the 'utilitarian' promotion of the 'common good'. Commenting on this, Clarke with Asquith say that: 'if respect for persons is more than an empty professional formula, it seems to commit social work to a deontological morality' (Clarke with Asquith, 1985, p. 77). In the context of the description of social work and social work values given in Part III, it is difficult to accommodate this statement from Clarke with Asquith, but like the earlier quotation from Wilkes ('values are not instrumental . . . but expressive of some ultimate conviction'), it seems to suggest that there is some 'absolute value truth' which is (or should be) fundamental and necessary to social work practice. Unfortunately, examination of this issue is often clouded and confused because, as for example in the quotation from Clarke with Asquith, such value talk is related to the often vague and mostly superficially used notion of 'professional' in the social work – ' 'professional guidelines', 'professional values', 'professional responsibilities', etc. To properly analyse what 'professional' means in the context of social work goes beyond the scope of this book, apart from a brief look at it in relation to the description of social work that has been developed.

Butrym (1976) lists four elements that are basic to professionalism in social work:

1 Service orientation – not putting the worker's interests before those of the client.
2 The social usefulness of social work.
3 Enhanced effectiveness.
4 Responsibilities held by professionals in trust for society.

This conception of social work is based on three assumptions:

(a) that there is a distance between the state and the professional
(b) that the profession has significant independence, and is apart from direct political control;
(c) that social work operates within only a broad social mandate.

According to Part III, this conception of social work as a profession is based on a myth, albeit a powerful one which, in order to establish social work with 'professional' status and credibility, ignores or at least seriously underestimates and misunderstands the relationship between social work and society. Social work is 'social' work and is practised directly and closely under social auspices, through a precise social mandate, and is subject to direct political control. Unlike other 'care' professions such as medicine and dentistry, social work is inextricably linked with the society which sanctions it, and which it serves.

What is significant from much of the use of the concept of 'professional' is that within it, social work values are conceptualized as being 'absolute', that is, they are conceptualized in a deontological way (see the quotations above from Wilkes and Clarke with Asquith). This is so to the extent that in as much as social work is a utilitarian enterprise, it is seen (if acknowledged at all) as being somehow separate from the 'absolute' value base of 'professional' social work practice. The argument here is that no such separation is possible. It is not possible to separate the 'form' of social work values from the way in which they work in practice.

Deontological and utilitarian values in context

While a deontologist might argue it is inherently right to maintain an elderly person in the community as long as possible, a utilitarian might justify placing the person in an institution on the grounds that, in the long run, this will result in less of a burden for the person's family (a desirable consequence) (Reamer, 1982, p. 17).

Whilst this example falls into the 'either – or' trap, it does illustrate the moral complexity of social work. Although social work may be described as a largely utilitarian enterprise, its values and how they work are not so readily described as being either utilitarian or deontological, as the example suggests. The 'reality' is that, although (as for example in the case illustration of Mrs M) a social worker would normally try to maintain an elderly person in the community for as long as possible, there may also come a time (as in the case of Mrs M) when the consequences of this on herself and others outweighs the elderly person's ability and right to remain in the community. It may be remembered that the social worker's role is to represent the interests and concerns of society as well as those of the individual, and within a discretionary space, mediate between the two. From this one cannot say, as according to the quotations from Clarke with Asquith, Wilkes and Reamer above, that the values of 'respect for persons' and client self-determination are 'absolute values', or are to be regarded or used deontologically. In the context in which local authority social work is practised this is not possible. The social worker is essentially mediating between the individual and society, and in this context the power or authority of social work values is essentially discretionary, and their 'absolute' work or applicability is subject to the interest and tolerance of society.

However, it would be equally false to claim (as in the quotation from Clarke with Asquith) that because of this, respect for persons is no more than an 'empty professional formula'. It is not empty because it is essential to the social work task of creating subjects, and without it there can be no social work. Without respect for persons (individuation) there can be no subject.

Without the 'subject' there is no social work. However, because social work is carried out under social auspices, in terms of determining the lives of individuals, social work values such as client self-determination are necessarily limited. Whilst one might in one sense describe as 'absolute', the social work task of creating subjects, the objective status of some individuals might in fact be greater than their subjective characteristics, and it is a part of the social work task to act according to society's mandate (which determines agency function) where this is the case, as it was in the case illustration of Mrs M.

Therefore, whilst respect for persons is essential to the creation of subjects, because of social workers' dependence on a 'social mandate', and the nature of the social work task itself, it does not provide the individual as client any rights within the client/social worker relationship.

Statements such as:

Social work is a professional activity. Implicit in its practice are ethical principles which prescribe the professional responsibility of the social worker. The primary objective of the code is make these implicit principles explicit for the protection of clients (BASW, 1975).

simply do not make sense when considered in the light of the argument above.

In the context of local authority social work, this quotation from BASW, and the earlier quotation from Reamer both fall short of understanding and relating to the complexity of the social work role in society.

References to 'clients' rights (BASW above), to 'professional' (BASW, Wilkes, Clarke with Asquith, Butrym) are problematical at the least because they are based on the idea of 'professional' being synonymous with 'independent' and 'autonomous'. This may be the case regarding some professions, but it certainly is not the case regarding social work. So to speak of values existing in the same vein is misguided.

To return to the quotation from Wilkes ('values are not instrumental . . . but expressive of some ultimate conviction'); one could argue that whilst values are instrumental to the task of creating subjects, and as such they may be held to be expressive of a central social work conviction; this conviction is also limited as it exists only within the boundaries of the extent to which society sanctions it. In other words this conviction is not ultimate in any 'absolute' sense, any more than the nature of a particular society is absolute. It is society's conviction to and interest in the subjective characteristics of certain people living on its margins that determines precisely what it means and how far it can be taken within social work practice.

It is clear from this that 'values in social work' is a considerably more complex and difficult area of study than has largely been hitherto acknowledged.

Traditionally 'values' have been studied and written about primarily in the context of the relationship between the social worker and client, mostly ignoring the relationship between the social worker and society.

However, in order to understand values, how they are used, and work in practice (within the social worker/client relationship) one has to acknowledge and examine the context in which this relationship takes place. That is, one has to examine and take account of the social worker's relationship with society, which itself sanctions, determines, defines, limits, and gives meaning to the social worker/client relationship.

12 Some Final Thoughts

The story so far . . .
The description and analysis of values in the preceeding chapters has
focused on two relationships – that between the social worker and the
individual/client, and that between the social worker and society/
agency. Social work values have been examined within these relationships, with 'how' they work being described as dependent on the
nature of the social work task and the social work role. This itself is
largely defined by society through agency function, which determines
and limits the nature of the social work task of creating 'subjects'. In
particular, by closely examining two case studies, we have seen how
self-determination (negative and positive freedom) is used in the social
worker/client relationship. From the analysis here, in terms of understanding 'values in social work', it is the social workers' relationship
with society/agency that is the most important one to consider in the
first instance as this determines the nature of the social worker's
relationship with the individual/client and hence, social work values.

Whilst this description and analysis does not of itself remove or
solve value dilemmas (in a prescriptive sense) around issues of what it
should be to 'respect persons'; the individual's right to be self-
determining; or issues around care and control, for example; it does
as far as these dilemmas are relevant to social work practice, place
them in the correct context for further examination.

The story to be continued . . .
One of the important things to emerge from this study is that in order
to examine and understand values in social work, one necessarily
engages in an examination of the nature of social work practice itself.
So, it is hoped that this examination of values has demonstrated the
importance and 'value' of focusing on social work values as a means to
understanding social work. As briefly stated in the Introduction
before Part I, social work is a value-laden activity. The basic idea of
having some form of social work embodies certain value judgements
made by society. It is society that determines that there are certain
categories of people who need certain kinds of attention and help.
The aims of social work, for example, the welfare of the individual
or group; the well-being of the whole community, are firmly rooted
in value assumptions made by society:

Not only do the aims of social work presuppose the basic values of our society, but also the specific judgements and decisions taken by the social worker in his attempt to further these aims are evaluative in turn (Downie and Loudfoot, 1978).

Given this situation a 'values' perspective could and should play an important role in our attempts to understand social work theory and practice, both descriptively (in terms of what it is) and prescriptively (in terms of how it may develop). This perspective though has to a large extent been ignored or avoided by social work researchers and theoreticians. Methodologically it presents many problems (which may be very apparent from this study itself), as 'values' do not lend themselves to measurement and quantification (see Peter Raynor, 1981 for an excellent critique/discussion on the limits of empricism in evaluating social work). However, value-based questions such as: who is the client; what is the client's good; what is the social worker's responsibility to his/her employing agency, society, his/her 'profession', the client and him/herself? - are essential in any examination and evaluation of social work. This is so whether examining social work in general, or a specific form of social work intervention with a specific client group. It is not sufficient simply to concentrate on the 'mechanics' or 'techniques' of social work because, as argued, social work is never 'purely a technical transaction' (Clarke with Asquith, 1985, p. 115) between social worker and client; it is 'socially constructed'.

It is obvious from the argument above that an understanding of values in social work, and an understanding of the nature of social work from a values perspective should play an important role in social work education, at all levels.

This is so, in at least two closely related ways. First, in terms of making sense of and understanding social works prescribed values (e.g. BASW's *Code of Ethics*). Second, by using a 'values perspective' in social work as a tool for examining the nature of social work practice, particularly in the context of the apparently conflicting roles of the social worker, for example, where the social worker is an agent of both care and control. Looking at the social work task in terms of relationships with the individual, and with society is, I think, a useful means by which to clarify the issues here.

The importance of an understanding of social work values and the responsibilities of social workers is recognized by CCETSW, for example in Paper 206 (1986). For this recognition to have any meaning though, social work training courses have to make the subject of values in social work a central component in the curriculum, rather than leaving it (as it is often the case) as an optional or fringe area of study, secondary to the 'mechanics' and 'techniques' of social work.

Finally, what I have written here is only 'a part of the story', in many ways only an introductory part. Awareness and consideration of social work's values, and of social work from a values perspective is growing. I hope my own contribution here constitutes a useful addition to this growing awareness by taking (if perhaps, somewhat riskily!) the subject firmly into the arena of social work practice – the arena of what social workers actually do.

Bibliography

Anderson, D., *Social Work and Mental Handicap*, Macmillan and BASW, 1982.

BASW, *A Code of Ethics for Social Work*, BASW, 1975.

BASW, *The Social Work Task*, BASW, 1977.

Berlin, I., 'Two Concepts of Liberty' in *Four Essays on Liberty*, pp. 121-134, Open University Press, 1969.

Bernstein, S., 'Self Determination: King or Citizen in the Realm of Values', in McDermott, 1975.

Biestek, F.P., *The Casework Relationship*, Allen and Unwin, 1961, 1974.

Budgen, R.P., 'A Critical Examination of the Principle of Self Determination in Social Work', unpub. PHD thesis, UEA, 1982.

Butrym, Z., *The Nature of Social Work*, Macmillan, 1976.

CCETSW, Paper 13: 'Values in Social Work', CCETSW, 1976.

CCETSW, Paper 20.3: 'Policies for Qualifying Training in Social Work: The Council's Propositions, CCETSW, 1985.

Channon, G., 'Values and Professional Social Work', *Australian Social Work*, 1974, 27, 1, pp. 5-14.

Clarke, C. with Asquith, S., *Social Work and Social Philosophy, A Guide for Practice*, Routledge & Kegan Paul, 1985.

Curnock, K. and Hardiker, P., *Towards Practice Theory: Skills and Methods in Social Assessments*, Routledge & Kegan Paul, 1979.

Davies, M., *The Essential Social Worker: A Guide to Positive Practice*, Heinemann Educational Books, 1981.

Downie, R.S. and Telfer, E., *Respect for Persons*, Allen and Unwin, 1969.

Downie, R.S. and Telfer, E., *Caring and Curing: A Philosophy of Medicine and Social Work*, Methuen, 1980.

Downie, R.S. and Loudfoot, E.M., 'Aim, Skill and Role in Social Work' in Timms and Watson, 1978.

Fairbairn, G. 'Responsibility in Social Work' in Watson D. (ed). 1985.

Fowler, D.A., 'Ends and Means' in Jones, 1975.

Hollis, F., 'Principles and Assumptions Underlying Casework Practice' in Younghusband, 1967.

Hollis, F., *Social Casework in Practice*, New York: Family Service Association of America, 1940.

Howe, D., 'Agency Function and Social Work Principles' in BJSW, 1979, 9, 1, pp. 29-47.

Husak, D., 'Paternalism and Autonomy' in *Philosophy and Public Affairs*, 1981, 10, pp. 27-46.

Jordan, B., 'The State isn't Abstract, it's a Social Worker Knocking on Someone's Door' in *Social Work Today*, 3 September 1984, pp. 10-14.

Johnson, T.J., 'The Professions in the Class Structure' in Scase, 1977.

Jones, H. (ed), *Towards a New Social Work*, Routledge & Kegan Paul, 1975.

Keith-Lucas, A., 'A Critique of the Principle of Client Self Determination', (1963) in McDermott, 1975.

Lane, L.C., 'The Aggressive to Preventative Casework', *Social Casework*, 1952, 33.

Levy, C.S., 'The Value Base of Social Work' in *Journal of Education for Social Work*, 1973, 9, pp. 34-42.

Levy, C.S., *Social Work Ethics*, Human Science Press, 1976.

Lindley, Richard, 'Strategic Family Therapy and Respect for People', 1984, unpublished.

McDermott, F.E., *Self Determination in Social Work*, Routledge & Kegan Paul, 1975.

McLeod, D. and Meyer, H.J., 'A Study of the Values of Social Workers' in Thomas, 1967.

Nokes, P., *The Professional Task in Welfare Practice*, Routledge & Kegan Paul, 1967.

Norman, A. *Rights and Risk – A Discussion Document on Civil Liberty in Old Age*, NCOP, 1980.

Paton, H.J., *The Moral Law*, Hutchinson, 1948.

Payne, M., The Code of Ethics, The Social Work Manager and the Organisation' in Watson, D. (ed), 1985.

Pearson, G., *The Deviant Imagination*, MacMillan, 1975.

Pearson G., 'The Politics of Uncertainty: A Study in the Socialization of the Social Worker' in Jones, 1975a.

Perlman, H.H., 'Self Determination: Reality or Illusion?' (1966) in McDermott, 1975.

Philp, M., 'Notes on the Form of Knowledge in Social Work' in *Sociological Review*, 1979, 27, pp. 83-111.

Plant, R., *Social and Moral Theory in Casework*, Routledge & Kegan Paul, 1970.

Pritchard, C. and Taylor, R., *Social Work: Reform or Revolution?* Routledge & Kegan Paul, 1978.

Pumphrey, M., *The Teaching of Values and Ethics in Social Work Education: A Project Report of the Curriculum Study*, Vol XIII, Council in Social Work Education USA, 1959.

Ragg, N., *People not Cases: A Philosophical Approach to Social Work*, Routledge & Kegan Paul, 1977.

Raynor, P., 'Evaluation with One Eye Closed: The Empiricist Agenda in Social Work Research' in BJSW, 1984, 14, pp. 1-10.

Reamer, F.G., *Ethical Dilemmas in Social Service*, Columbia HN 245
University Press, 1982.

Scase, R. (ed) *Industrial Society, Class, Cleavage and Control*, Allen
and Unwin, 1977.

Seebohm Report, *Report of the Committee on Local Authority and
Allied Social Services*, HMSO, 1968.

Smalley, R., *Theory for Social Work Practice*, Columbia University
Press, 1967.

Statham, D., *Radicals in Social Work*, Routledge & Kegan Paul, 1978.

Thomas, E.J. (ed) *Behavioural Science for Social Workers*, The Free
Press, New York, 1967.

Timms, N., *Social Casework*, Routledge & Kegan Paul, 1964.

Timms, N., *Social Work: An Outline for Intending Students*, Routledge
& Kegan Paul, 1970.

Timms, N. and Timms R., *Perspectives in Social Work*, Routledge &
Kegan Paul, 1977.

Timms, N., *Social Work Values: An Enquiry*, Routledge & Kegan
Paul, 1983.

Timms, N. and Watson, D., *Philosophy in Social Work*, Routledge &
Kegan Paul, 1978.

Titmuss, R.M., *Essays on the Welfare State*, Allen and Unwin, 1958.

Vigilante, J., 'Between Values and Science: Education for the Professional During a Moral Crisis or is Proof Truth?' *Journal of Education
for Social Work*, 1974, 10, pp. 107-15.

Warham, J., *An Open Case: The Organisational Context of Social
Work*, Routledge & Kegan Paul, 1977.

Warnock, M. (ed) *Utilitarianism*, Collins, 1962.

Watson, D., *Caring for Strangers*, Routledge & Kegan Paul, 1980.

Watson, D. (ed) *A Code of Ethics for Social Work, the 2nd Step*,
Routledge & Kegan Paul, 1985.

Whittington, K., 'Self-Determination Re-examined' in McDermott,
1975.

Wilkes, R., *Social Work with Undervalued Groups*, Tavistock, 1981.

Winnicott, C., *Child Care and Social Work*, Caldicote Press, 1964. HQ 769

Younghusband, E. (ed) *Social Work and Social Values*, Allen and
Unwin, 1967.

ndex